UNLEARNING

Changing Your Beliefs and Your Classroom With UDL

D1571814

ALLISON POSEY
KATIE NOVAK

CAST Professional
Publishing

UNTIL LEARNING HAS NO LIMITS™

Paperback ISBN 978-1-930583-44-3
Ebook ISBN 978-1-930583-47-4

Library of Congress Control Number 2019949547

Design and illustrations by Lindie Johnson

Bulk discounts available: For details, email publishing@cast.org or visit www.castpublishing.org.

Published by:
CAST Professional Publishing
an imprint of CAST, Inc.
Wakefield, Massachusetts, USA

Allison

To Griffin and Ella—to the Oort cloud and back.

Katie

Always to Lon, Torin, Aylin, Brec, and Boden. The five of you are my world.

Contents

Three Teaspoons of Lemon Juice
Not an Introduction Because Not Everyone Reads Those

For a moment, just consider all the many innovations that have been introduced in your teaching career—the strategies, the frameworks, and the curriculum unveiled in professional development and never heard from again. Yeah, you know the ones. How many of those actually transformed your teaching practices?

Many of our current teaching practices work well and inspire a new generation of students to thrive in our communities; however, there are still too many students who do not succeed in school. According to the National Center for Education Statistics, the percentage of fourth-grade students performing at or above the proficient achievement level in 2015 was 36 percent. According to research, 66 percent of surveyed students reported being bored in every class or at least every day in school. Of these students, 98 percent claimed that the material being taught was the main reason for their boredom, 81 percent thought their subject material was uninteresting, and two out of three students found that the material lacked relevance (Yazzie-Mintz, 2010). What would it take to change our practices so that we are able to reach and engage every student? How long would something like that take? How much would we have to change?

Consider the story of the great Captain Lancaster, shared by Everett Rogers (1962). In the early 1400s, when seafaring was booming, countless men on his ships were lost to an illness we now know of as scurvy. Many other ship crews suffered the same demise.

We can only imagine that physicians and captains were scurrying to find an elixir that would save their sailors. In the case study, Everett does not go into how Captain Lancaster happened upon a cure for scurvy, but he did. He then set up a study to test it. Lancaster had four ships headed out for exploration, so he took the opportunity to select one group for treatment. The men on that ship were lucky enough to ingest three teaspoons of lemon juice a day to ward off the illness. Every one of the crew survived the journey.

On the other three ships, the control ships, the sailors were not given lemon juice. Halfway through the journey, more than half of them died. A hundred went out. Fifty went overboard. The loss of life was so debilitating that the treatment ship had to come to the rescue. These sailors, armed with lemon juice, had to man the remaining ships just to bring them back home.

Think about the logic of this innovation. If you want all of your sailors to survive, you bring lemon juice on board. If you want many to die, you don't. Naturally, Captain Lancaster celebrated this discovery and shared it with everyone he knew. Sadly, it did not catch on. In fact, even though some innovative sailors did replicate Lancaster's findings, it took two hundred years for the British Navy to endorse the treatment: 1.6 million gallons of lemon juice later, between 1795 and 1815, eradicated scurvy (Tannahill, 1989).

In the field of education, we have our own experiment going. If we think of one of the statistics from the start of this chapter, of a hundred students in a class only thirty-six will learn to read at grade level. If we reflect on other schoolwide statistics, for every hundred students with disabilities in America, only sixty-one are educated with their general education peers for 80 percent of the school day.

What if we, the authors of this book, told you that we had a three-teaspoon equivalent to learning: Universal Design for Learning (UDL). UDL is like the lemon juice on board a ship. It is a way to approach teaching and learning to reach and engage every student in our classroom. Students who live in areas where schools or individual teachers adopt and implement UDL are on the equivalent of the treatment ship. They have access to lemon juice. Everyone else—we are setting out to sail. But we do not want change in our learning environments to take two hundred years.

As teachers, we worked states apart, yet we shared a common goal: we believed we could reach every one of our students. We believed that all students deserve to be empowered to drive their own learning journey. And we held high expectations for them. We didn't necessarily know how to do this, we just knew that we wanted to. However, we also experienced how often teaching meant following a curriculum that was designed for a mythical average learner. We acknowledged that our classrooms didn't work for every student, but we didn't always know what other choices we had. Does this resonate with you?

The universe brought us together to learn about UDL as a framework that could help us design learning environments for all. At that time, we saw the power and possibility of reaching and engaging every student. Our challenge was that the transformation would mean letting go of most of what we had learned about how to teach.

From our work with educators from all disciplines, ages, and contexts around the world, we know that teachers want what is best for their students and we hear about the great lengths they go to in trying to reach every learner. We also hear consistently about the how hard it is to teach the tremendous range of students in their classrooms. The theory behind UDL resonates as a way to reach all of our students, yet it is the implementation of UDL that often presents challenges. Educators want to know: What are the first steps; what does UDL look like; how will I know if I'm on the right track; and do we know whether it works? If UDL is the "lemon juice" that can transform our teaching and learning environments so that they meet the needs of all students, why isn't it being applied by every educator in the world already?

We have colleagues who have implemented UDL and have experienced exponential success: increased graduation rates, a tenfold increase in all student cohorts on state standardized tests, an increase in the number of students taking AP exams, and decreased special education referrals and out-of-school suspensions. When we see and hear of these incredible shifts as a result of UDL, we feel like Captain Lancaster probably felt and want to share UDL with everyone.

However, we have also found that sometimes, like the British government, even when teachers learn about UDL and believe in its power to transform their teaching and learning environments, many still do not change. We do not think that this is because educators are unwilling to make change, but perhaps because they may not think there is a strong reason to change, or perhaps they do not necessarily know the first steps to take. We have wrestled with this dilemma for years, trying many different approaches to teach and model UDL. We have come to understand that for all the research, brain science, and best practices that are behind UDL as a way to reach all students without differentiating learning at every turn, there is an elephant in the room. Most teachers, including us, have a hard time integrating new learning.

Why is changing what we do so hard? We came to understand that to change how we think about teaching, how we manage our classrooms, and how we develop curriculum, we must *unlearn*. Yes, unlearn. In a profession that spends so much time thinking about learning, the process of unlearning is what needs to happen before real change can happen.

Wait, what?

Resist the temptation to throw this book out the window or up against a wall. Hear us out. This unlearning process has been such a transformative experience for us, even as so-called UDL experts, that we want to invite you on this journey. This journey will take you along a route to design learning experiences that not only are accessible for students but that challenge them to become more autonomous and self-directed in their learning. We have seen student agency increase and engagement skyrocket when UDL is implemented. We have observed teachers transformed by UDL who celebrated their learning journeys along the way. But this isn't just a book about UDL. It is a book that recognizes the fact that we know we aren't meeting the needs of all students and we know that we can.

The process of unlearning as part of the learning process has been well documented. What is unique about this book is that we will support the process of unlearning using UDL. UDL is a tool that guides the design of learning environments to support the anticipated variability of our students, to help us be goal-directed and to prioritize engagement, and to ensure that every individual knows how to be an expert learner who is motivated, knowledgeable, and strategic. We will use this process to guide educators to unlearn some of their tried-and-true techniques in order to support the wide range of students in our classrooms.

If our classrooms and systems were working for every single student, we wouldn't need to unlearn and change our current practices. However, as both research and our own personal experience suggest, the system is not working for too many. We knew this before we learned about UDL, but it didn't feel like there was much we could do about it. When we recognized the barriers inherent in our classrooms, there was an overwhelming sense of urgency to make changes. We recognized that it was up to us to eliminate barriers and to engage every student. We even started to wonder about many of our students who seemed successful in school—how many were just compliant with the routines and not fully invested in learning? And what could we do? To be honest, it felt overwhelming at times. As much as we believed and wanted each student to thrive in our classrooms, we each had moments where we felt like it would be a lot easier to give up. And at times, we did give up, sat in the teachers' room, and felt like we were going to cry.

We hear the problems teachers face around the country, which range from students who don't care about school, parents who don't support learning, or mental illnesses we aren't qualified to address. We sometimes blame the system and lament the lack of resources, professional development, and administrative support. These are real barriers. We know you face them. And we see you. But it's important to know that, despite the barriers, we can still inspire and motivate students and leave them better than when they met us. That is our calling, and we must keep that at the center of everything we do. Once you unlearn ineffective practices, we contend that you will be closer to the teacher you want to be—the one who connects with students, is intentional about instructional moves, and inspires students to become architects of their own learning. This transformation, however, is not so much a result of learning about UDL as of unlearning ineffective traditional practices.

Interestingly, the greatest barrier to unlearning can be the education that we received through our own school experiences, through college and teacher preparation programs, in graduate school, and through our professional development. From these experiences, we know plenty about teaching and learning—but some of it is no longer relevant. For example, through our own graduate education and professional training, we both learned a "tried-and-true" writing technique—the five-paragraph essay.

First, to be clear, there is such a thing as a five-paragraph essay, but there are also four-paragraph, 17-paragraph, and 22-paragraph essays. Advanced, confident writers understand that the number of paragraphs isn't as important as whether the writing is organized appropriately for the task. However, as educators we are often still taught to use this method as a best practice, a "tried-and-true" formula for teaching students to learn how to write.

And yet, college- and career-ready standards require us to move away from counting paragraphs and, instead, teach students to focus on the task, the intended audience, and the purpose of writing. Sometimes it is appropriate to address a prompt using five paragraphs, but there is no rule that essays have to be bound to a scripted format or paragraph count. But, hey, we are both guilty of assigning many a five-paragraph essay because that is supposed to be a best practice.

What if we were to think about teaching writing like cooking. It is valuable to start with a recipe, or writing instruction, that outlines predictable formulas, but then provide scaffolding to move students away from those templates. Great writers don't follow formulas, just as great chefs don't follow recipes. They may keep a recipe in the back of their mind, but then they use their own style to make magic. Yet many teachers don't move away from teaching the five-paragraph essay (it took us both a while) even though not all students seem to benefit from this approach.

In short, if we want to learn how to teach all of our students today, we have to unlearn many of those teaching practices that are no longer effective. We do not mean you need to ditch all your best practices—but you will likely come away from this book thinking about how you teach, why you teach, and what you can teach in a new way.

In this book, we articulate the transformation that can take place in order to develop student-driven, engaging, rigorous learning experiences, and UDL can be a tool to support your journey to achieve that (See Appendix A for resources to teach you more about UDL.) The Unlearning Cycle can be used to adjust some of the habits and routines that may not be working for student learning. We have developed the Unlearning Cycle to support educators seeking to implement UDL in their practice. It is important to note that these do not necessarily occur in a linear progression, but include the following essential elements:

The Unlearning Cycle

1. Understand variability
2. Know your goals
3. Transform tried-and-true techniques
4. Prioritize engagement
5. Scaffold expert learning

We present a new mindset for teaching that aligns with what we currently know about the learning brain and that integrates new tools and techniques to help support your Unlearning Cycle. This book is for teachers and the professionals who support them. It is for educators who are interested in UDL but have not been able to transform practice to increase the outcomes of all learners.

As an educator, you can go through the process individually, with a team in a professional learning community, or as a school or district. We recognize that you are bombarded with professional development requirements and we hope that this book will offer you an easy, efficient, yet deeply thoughtful way to transform your practice not only to reach all your learners but to intentionally design for meaningful, challenging learning.

In this book, we will take you through the Unlearning Cycle in two ways. The first invites you to think about yourself and your teaching practices. This self-assessment and reflection is critical to understanding the process of unlearning as it is not only applicable to your classroom instruction but can be generalized to parenting, cooking,

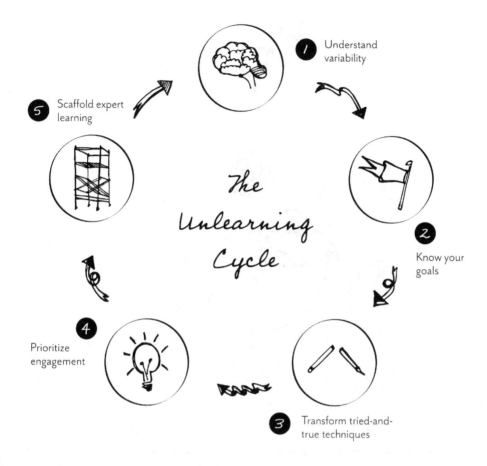

The Unlearning Cycle

1 Understand variability

2 Know your goals

3 Transform tried-and-true techniques

4 Prioritize engagement

5 Scaffold expert learning

exercising, leadership, and more—you name it. It is tempting to pick up a professional book and want concrete steps for action you can implement tomorrow. Don't worry—those are coming. But first we must take the time to think about all we have learned about teaching and learning, and then unlearn it. Taking time for self-assessment and reflection is critical for learning and personalized goal-setting. Beginning with you, the reader, is critical to this process. Through this process, you will gain an understanding of the power of unlearning, will better understand why change is challenging; and, most importantly, you will have all the tools to adopt the mindset you need to transform your practice.

Once we have taken you through a reflective process, you will be ready for action! We will get to strategies and to necessary steps for UDL implementation. We will discuss how to design lessons that reduce barriers that often prevent students from succeeding. We will offer strategies for how to partner with students to foster expert learning. As tempting as it may be, starting with application won't result in the

outcomes you are hoping for. We must first transform ourselves in order to transform our systems. We have to unravel old practices so we have the capacity to create more effective ones. The unlearning process is one of reflection, destruction, and change, but it is also one of learning and growth.

As you read this book, consider pondering the questions provided for reflection, discussing its ideas with peers in a professional learning group, or writing a blog to share with educators across the world (don't forget #UDLchat and #UDLUnlearning). By jotting down Sketchnotes or thoughts in a journal or in the space at the end of each chapter, you can also ask your own questions about your teaching practices. Think of this book as your interactive guide to unlearning and to your UDL transformation.

Thank you for taking this journey with us. Our students are absolutely worth our efforts.

Before you dive into this book, think for a moment about a time when you experienced something in a new way. For example, consider the first time you used Lyft or Uber, tried Siri, or saw a Fitbit or Apple watch.

- What was your initial experience/impression of this new way of doing things?
- What were the trade-offs/benefits of that change?
- What parts of the old experience do you still want to hold onto?

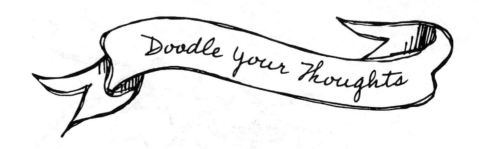

1   Apples and Buffets

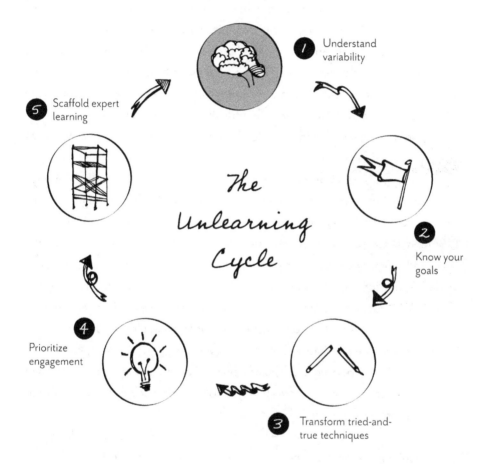

The Unlearning Cycle

1. Understand variability
2. Know your goals
3. Transform tried-and-true techniques
4. Prioritize engagement
5. Scaffold expert learning

Assumptions, Apples, and What's in Our Way

This is a fact: when there is no light there is no color. For example, when you look at an apple, it looks red because wavelengths of light are reflected from the apple onto the cone photoreceptors in your eyes. You perceive the redness because of the reflection of that light. Without the light, there is no color—literally nothing is reflected onto the cones of your eyes, so there is nothing to perceive: no electrical signal goes to your brain; nothing is stimulated. However, regardless of these scientific facts, individuals who have been placed in a completely dark room, a room where absolutely no light can enter, still claim to see an apple as being red. They know that there is no light in the room, and they have learned the science that explains how, in an absence of light, there is no color. However, they still claim to see color! They use reasoning such as, "My eyes must not have adjusted to the dark yet so I could still see the redness," or "Some light must somehow have gotten into the room." They still see the apple as red even though it is impossible. Why is this (Grotzer, 2012)?

Our everyday experiences are critical to how we perceive, understand, and engage with the world around us. They can influence how we learn and whether or not we take action. Based on our experiences, we have learned that apples are red (sometimes green, if it's a Granny Smith). We have learned to pick, eat, and cut apples. We know that if we add a little lemon juice to an apple, it does not brown as quickly.

Neurologically, when we look at an apple, photons of light reflect off it, stimulate cone photoreceptors of our eyes, and the resultant signal is sent through the optic nerve to the multiple brain networks, including the occipital lobe of the brain. Here, color- and shape-sensitive networks perceive the redness and roundness of the apple, and memory centers in the temporal lobes recall that this object is called "apple." Frontal lobe networks understand that we could plan to hold and bring the apple to our mouths to eat. From all of our years of experiences and interactions with apples, we have constructed neural networks that know apples. And typically, our experiences with them include a light source—even at night we are rarely completely void of light. Our experiences of apples being red are so strong that we still claim to see a red color even when there literally *is* no red color. So what might it take to unlearn that apples are not red?

New learning and change can be really difficult. They take energy and deliberate effort, requiring that we build new models of understanding and change what we perceive and how we act. New learning requires persistence, a willingness to trade old explanations for new ones and to try new things—to get out of our comfort zone. Even when we know better and are trying to change, we still tend to fall back on our previous assumptions and prior beliefs. We stick to an old habit and routine, even when it contradicts what we now know to be true. For instance, we say that the apple is red even in a completely dark room, even after learning about how light and color work.

In our classrooms, our teaching routines and habits can be really hard to change as well. At a recent presentation, we modeled a UDL lesson as if fellow educators were high school students. They were given three options to build background knowledge of imagery: working with the presenter in a small group, reviewing the textbook section, or watching a short video tutorial. One teacher was flabbergasted by these suggestions. He said, "But every student has to use the textbook—we need them to read." Pushing back, we asked, "But, why?" He couldn't come up with an answer other than to say he had just used the textbook for so many years that he couldn't consider another option. We get it. Change is very hard.

English teachers may love the experience of assigning the same novel to a whole class; math teachers assign homework asking every student to complete all of the same problems. In physical education, all students run the mile, play dodgeball, or must try to learn to play team sports like basketball and ultimate frisbee—even though no specific sport is mandated in the standards. Science teachers host fairs with three-paneled posters.

Based on our years of experience, both as learners and as educators, we fall back on patterns and methods that may not reflect our current understanding or the research of learning and the brain. It is as though we get into the context of the classroom and fall into the routines of a teacher as one who delivers information to students. We fall back on old ways of assigning worksheets and presenting lectures, even when we know that these methods are not working for all students. Perhaps we think, "Well, this is how I've done it before and it turned out alright." We fall back on old "tried-and-true" techniques. We think the apple is red because in most contexts that is what we have experienced. We cannot imagine that it has no color. However, the apple was actually never red! As we deepen our understanding about color and light, we can see how misguided some of our perceptions and assumptions are. Similarly, current research about the brain can help us recognize where some current practices may need to be redesigned.

The Learning Buffet Analogy

Imagine that we are going to have you all over to eat dinner tonight and that we are serving homemade Mexican lasagna. It is smothered with cheese and filled with meat, salsa, onions, black beans, and corn. Now some of you probably already thinking, "I'm not going to eat this lasagna, no matter how delicious it is described to be." You may be polite, pick at some bites of food, but you will be left unsatisfied at the end of the meal. Some of you may not eat at all. Some of you may not even show up for the dinner party, knowing that you won't enjoy the fare. We might reflect on how picky some of you are, try to be a cheerleader for some of you, defend our choice to serve lasagna, noting all of its benefits and wonders; one of us might even try to sit next to you and feed you bite by bite: "You can do it. I know you can!" However, by the end of the night, we are probably exhausted. There may be proud moments remembering those who really enjoyed the lasagna, yet feelings of disappointment at or frustration with the handful of you who did not eat.

What if we try a few new strategies the next time we host a dinner party? For example, we might make three lasagnas: one with meat, one with no cheese, and one with just veggies (but who has time for that?). Or we might make a plain pasta as a cheap and easy modification of the lasagna. We might hand out Lactaid to those who cannot eat lactose-filled cheese. But this still doesn't quite work.

Imagine that instead we approach the dinner through the lens of a buffet. This buffet, of course, starts by identifying a clear purpose for the meal, perhaps that "All guests will enjoy a *well-balanced meal* at the party." We define what we mean by "well-balanced," and then we can create a buffet of options that *each dinner guest* can choose from in order to create their own meal. We open up the kitchen cabinets and bring out some new options that perhaps we wouldn't have put in the lasagna but that could work for some of you (Tabasco anyone?). Using this method we don't have to pre-make multiple lasagnas or even know the dietary requirements of each of you (which might vary from meal-to-meal due to the magic of variability). How many more eaters can engage and achieve the goal when we take the buffet approach?

The buffet approach is proactive and assumes that people who are dining will bring with them a range of eating preferences for any particular meal. The buffet approach does not label the eaters but enables each to make choices that align with their eating goals. Some may have just eaten already and need to make different choices than they might have ordinarily (context matters).

Similarly, in lesson design, the UDL approach is more like the buffet and anticipates a range of learning preferences for any particular lesson. It also recognizes that within each lesson, those preferences will vary based on different factors: for example, a student may have just had a fight with a friend, not had any lunch, or not slept well the night before. Each of these circumstances can impact the preferences a student may make on a given day. We can use the UDL Guidelines (see Appendix B) to plan a "learning buffet" for our students, offering flexible pathways they can choose from as they work to achieve the lesson goal. We can work with students to co-construct the buffet to be sure their learning is "well-balanced."

While the buffet is a strong analogy for thinking about UDL, UDL is not just about offering choices. The UDL Guidelines are a tool for helping to select intentional learning choices to ensure that all learners can access and participate in meaningful, robust learning opportunities. The Guidelines suggest three broad ways of offering flexibility in our lessons by providing options for Engagement, Representation, and Action and Expression. Think of these as comparable to the four main food groups: proteins, vegetables, fruits, grains—but for learning. For any learning experience ask: What options are there for students to engage, to build background, and to show what they know? This helps us put together an effective "learning buffet." However, the buffet is just the beginning of the UDL journey. If you need a refresher on the UDL Guidelines, see the section below.

When faced with a buffet, how do you balance what you want to eat, what you need to eat, and the logistics (how much time you have to eat, what you're doing

Overview of the UDL Guidelines

The UDL Guidelines are based on three principles: providing multiple means of Engagement, Representation, and Action and Expression. These three UDL principles align with three broad learning networks in the brain: affective, recognition, and strategic networks.

UDL Engagement Principle. Engagement is essential for learning. When we are interested, we focus and persist in our work. Indeed, we might become so engrossed in an activity that we don't notice that time has passed or that we have not eaten! With UDL, the goal is to develop intrinsic motivation for students to be purposeful and motivated in developing their interests, in sustaining their effort and persistence, and in self-regulating through challenges.

UDL Representation Principle. Recognition networks are activated from inputs perceived from the environment. We know that students will have a broad range of background experiences that influence what they pay attention to. UDL guides us to reflect on how there are options to perceive the pertinent information, gain necessary language and symbols, and build comprehension.

UDL Action and Expression Principle. Strategic networks are important for how we show what we know. We know there will be a full range of physical ability, expression and communication, and executive functions in our classrooms: some students will know how to take the steps to craft loquacious essays on a topic, while others will hardly write a word but share deep understandings in a discussion.

To examine the UDL Guidelines and checkpoints, see Appendix B.

---

later, etc.)? In the buffet example, we may lay out an amazing spread of noodles, veggies, meats and tofu, and cheeses in individual ramekins. At the end of the table, we may have brownies, cookies, and a pitcher of sangria. We encourage you, as our guests, to choose, do, and then review (Anderson, 2016). But before you choose, we remind you to consider what you want to eat, what you need to eat to be healthy and not feel sick, and also to consider how much time you have to eat, what you're doing later in the day, and so on. Some of you may have another dinner party to get to, so even though you're interested in a full ramekin and you need to carbo-load for a road race the following day, it's not the best choice. Instead, you decide on a salad because it's the best choice considering your interests, needs, and the logistics involved. You continue to reflect on and have clarified your goals for the meal and you have learned over time what it means to be an "expert" eater—one who knows how to make these nuanced choices.

UDL design encourages a subtle but profound shift, in that each diner is able to make choices based on the goal. However, we hear from educators that students may not make good choices and that it may even be overwhelming for them to make a choice. We need to start to support students to become more "expert" consumers and to build more of a community of collaboration around high-level, goal-directed "eating." This approach will take work to prepare! It may take more time, for example, at the start of the school year to establish some routines and skills.

In *Learning to Choose, Choosing to Learn*, teacher Mike Anderson (2016) focuses on supporting students in making effective choices about their learning. Empowering learners to self-reflect, make choices, and learn from those choices eliminates many of the barriers that prevent educators from embracing the UDL framework.

First, students will not be primed to make choices unless teachers proactively create "conditions of nurture." In UDL, our goal is to create classrooms that minimize threats and distractions. These threats and distractions can be eliminated through Anderson's conditions of nurture, which are safety, inclusion, and collaboration. Putting in the effort to reflect on your learning environment "buffet" is critical in determining whether the conditions for learning are optimal.

There will be challenges to letting students choose. Some may always choose the same pathway, others may struggle to make a choice. There is frequently concern that students will always choose the "easy" way. Making great choices is a skill, so it's possible that students won't make the best choices all the time, but it is our responsibility to create opportunities for them to reflect and realize that their choice wasn't effective. It is also an opportunity to empower students to provide us with feedback on the types of choices that will help them make better choices.

Conditions of nurture "prime the pump" and prepare students for the process of making choices, a process that Anderson refers to as "choose, do, review." When we, as educators, provide a buffet for students, we may encourage them to choose and do, but do we take the necessary time to provide options for students to monitor their progress and self-reflect on their choice? Sometimes the perceived "easy way" is actually strategic and could be the best choice for the student.

How can we transform our classroom environments to be more like buffets that help us reach more of the variability of our students? How can we help students become more autonomous in making their learning choices and ensure that they are, for the most part, effective choices? It sounds so simple, yet it is actually really challenging. This is going to require that we unlearn some of our previous teaching methods—starting with how we label students.

Where Are You Now?
Questions for Reflection:

- Draw out your classroom. Where is the current "buffet" of options for students?
- How do you already provide options for students to engage with the learning experience, to build background, and to show what they know?

From Labels to Variability

Physicians in the 1800s recommended that their tuberculosis patients collapse an infected lung by puncturing it and then told them to go to the countryside to breathe fresh air. Today, if a physician were to suggest this treatment, we would be shocked and refuse to be treated! Of course, we know more about tuberculosis and the lungs now and expect physicians to have updated their practices. What are some of the old ways of thinking about learning and the brain that we need to be sure are no longer part of our teaching practices?

Brain research has shown beyond any doubt that each human brain is unique: variability is the rule (Meyer, Rose, & Gordon, 2014; Rose, 2016). Even identical twins have incredibly different brains. We do not have isolated learning styles; for example, there are no "kinesthetic" or "visual" learning styles in the brain (Willingham, 2018). With new imaging tools, we are able to see just how interconnected and active the brain is. Even reading a simple word such as "dog" activates the whole brain "in a rich symphony of back and forth processing between many areas of the brain" (Dale & Hagren, 2017).

How many of us have labeled ourselves as being a "visual" learner or labeled a student as being a "left-brained" thinker? These labels are outdated, and we need to realign our thinking about our students' learning to this more complex concept of variability. "Variability" is the term used to describe just how unique and varied our brains are. No two learners ever activate the same pathways in the brain. One student with a label of "autism" will have a unique brain pattern and learning needs totally different from those of another student with the same label. While labels may be an important aspect of identity, people are so much more complex than labels that may define them. When we are focused only on labels, and not the whole person, we run the risk of having a fixed mindset or making false assumptions about our learners.

While the concept of variability often resonates with educators, what does this really mean for our classrooms? First, it means that we cannot label students in a fixed way. Instead, a useful way to shift our thinking is to use the jagged learning profile (Rose, 2016). The jagged learning profile represents a broader way of describing the full range of our strengths and weaknesses. It also takes into consideration the important role played by context, or the environment, in how these strengths and weaknesses are highlighted. For example, think about a physical jagged learning profile of an athlete in training. We should consider several factors, such as strength, endurance, effort, diet, and mindset. Each athlete will have his or her own unique jagged profile for each of these and, importantly, this profile can shift based on the context. A swimmer who has remarkable endurance and speed in the water may seem uncoordinated and slow when running on land. Another player may have great persistence and mindset in practice but may shut down and get easily frustrated during match play. The context really matters.

We can use the nine UDL Guidelines to help us think about different dimensions of a jagged profile: interest, persistence, self-regulation, perception, language and symbols, comprehension, physical action, expression and communication, and executive functions. For example, in a science classroom, a student's jagged profile might include a high interest level, robust background knowledge, and strong vocabulary; however, she may not persist in dealing with challenging problems or manage her time well (executive functions). Importantly, this profile may shift when this same student goes to another classroom or when we move to a different unit. That is how the context intersects with the jagged profile. (Note that there are other ways to develop a student's jagged learning profile than using the UDL Guidelines. For example, you may ask students to self-reflect on their study skills, background knowledge, vocabulary, and presentation skills as a means to highlight the variability in your classroom!)

When we present information in one way or expect that students will work in the same way and at the same time, we are not recognizing the variability of their jagged profiles. When we label students in a fixed grouping, we are not considering how the context can influence the learning experience. We encourage you to reflect on your classroom practices in light of this understanding of variability and context.

Consider your own jagged profile: Where are your strengths and weaknesses? How do these align with background experiences you have had? How do these strengths and weaknesses shift based on the context, and how do they influence your teaching preferences or environment? (Try the "Doodle Your Own Variability" exercise on page 11.) For example, perhaps you feel very skilled at presenting lectures that are engaging and well organized. However, when your supervisor is attending your lecture, that could shift the context for you and you may feel less engaged or organized. Perhaps you don't feel comfortable with technology, but if you have a co-teacher or technology specialist in the room with you, it might make a shift in your ability.

These two key ideas from brain science are essential to understanding how to move forward with UDL implementation: (1) Variability. The brain is made up of complex interconnected networks that are unique to each individual. We do not have one fixed learning profile or style of learning, but instead have diverse jagged profiles; (2) Based on the context, those profiles may shift.

Where Are You Now?
Questions for Reflection:

- How is thinking about students' variability and their jagged profiles of strengths and challenges in different classroom contexts different from labeling students or having lessons that must be completed in the same way and at the same time?
- How does the context, or the environment, contribute to the strengths and weaknesses of your students? Of you?

Discrepant Events

It was in a mundane moment in an ice-cream store one evening that a teacher had an "aha!" moment of clarity that deepened his understanding of UDL. After looking at the array of ice-cream choices and toppings, he ordered a dairy-free chocolate-chip cone with sprinkles. Suddenly, he realized: "Wait a minute, I am not lactose intolerant, but I just ordered the dairy-free option. What if I was told that I could only order this kind because I had a dairy allergy? I would be so angry!" He continued to reflect on how this was like the approach he uses in his classroom, "I realized that I only allow some of my students to use certain options, perhaps students who receive Special Education services or who are English Language Learners—and I am usually the one who makes the selection. I tell students what level they are on or what tools to use. Why don't I open up the options for everyone and let them be part of the choice?"

From this discrepant event in the ice-cream store, this educator shifted his thinking about the design of his lessons and how they could be more like an ice-cream buffet and include more student voice and choice. These "aha!" moments, or discrepant events, are important opportunities for conceptual change. It is when, suddenly, a lightbulb goes off and we realize that what we thought previously is no longer accurate. The conceptual change approach was first described in science

Doodle your Own Variability

	Low	Average	High
Interest			
Persistence			
Self-regulation			
Perception			
Language & Symbols			
Comprehension			
Physical Action			
Communication			
Executive Functions			

Context 1

	Low	Average	High
Interest			
Persistence			
Self-regulation			
Perception			
Language & Symbols			
Comprehension			
Physical Action			
Communication			
Executive Functions			

Context 2

	Low	Average	High
Interest			
Persistence			
Self-regulation			
Perception			
Language & Symbols			
Comprehension			
Physical Action			
Communication			
Executive Functions			

Context 3

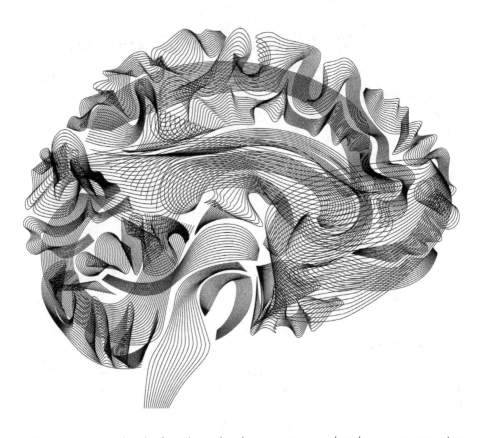

when scientists realized, often through a discrepant event, that they must start using the new paradigm and abandon the old one (Posner, Strike, Hewson, & Gertzog, 1982). In short, it can happen with us in education too. These discrepant events are valuable moments to help motivate us to unlearn what we previously held to be true.

Look for small moments in your teaching practice to think about trying something new related to this understanding of variability and context. Perhaps it will be when you start to create a graphic organizer for your "weak students" and realize that there will be "variability" in student organizational skills and that many students might benefit from the graphic organizer. So you ditch the "weak student" label and make the graphic organizer available for any student to use. It is when a teacher allows an audiobook for a student with dyslexia, but then recognizes that it can help many different students, from those who may be working late at night and have tired eyes to those who may listen to the assignment on a walk. It is when teachers give students the opportunity to use note-taking apps or Sketchnotes during class, and as a result their engagement and achievement skyrocket. (Hey, maybe Cornell notes aren't for everyone.) All of these examples shift the focus to designing and changing the environment with flexible options—and do not label students in fixed ways.

The Unlearning Cycle

At this point in the Unlearning Cycle, we start to see that there is learner variability, not fixed learning styles. To support this variability, the UDL approach is more like setting a learning buffet of options than creating different "meals" for each student. This is the stage at which educators often get enthusiastic about setting a learning buffet for their students and may start to offer lots of choices (usually too many at first!). Other educators enjoy learning the brain science of variability but don't make any changes to their classroom practice. Some claim that UDL is not anything new but just another "initiative" that will come and go. In our work with educators, we frequently hear comments such as these at this point:

- "This is great, I'm on board and already do UDL."
- "I'm going to try to provide students lots of options in my lesson."
- "UDL sounds just like good teaching. This is nothing new."

Regardless of which of these ideas resonates most with you, there is typically no change in teaching practices at this point in UDL implementation. That is because there is still more unlearning to do! Understanding the ideas of the "learning buffet," variability, and context is the first critical step.

Where Are You Now?
Questions for Reflection:

- How does the ice-cream story resonate with you? Have you had similar experiences that have caused an "aha!" or discrepant event that shifted your thinking?
- What resonates so far in your learning about UDL, variability, and context? What is a first step you can take?

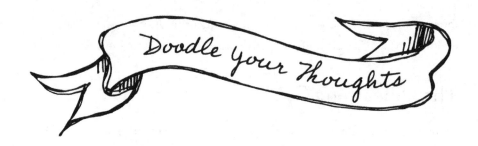

2 The UDL Road Trip

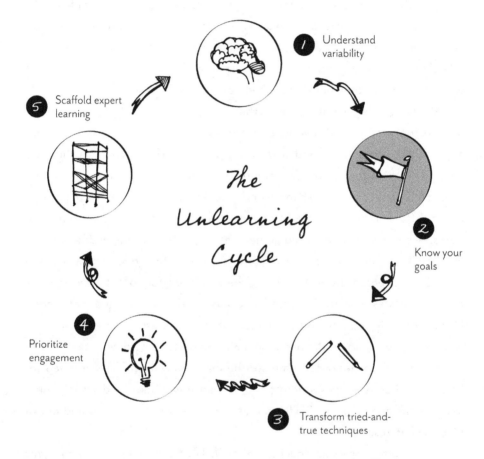

The Unlearning Cycle

1. Understand variability
2. Know your goals
3. Transform tried-and-true techniques
4. Prioritize engagement
5. Scaffold expert learning

The Amazing-ness of Each Student

We have been lucky enough to teach students who have transformed us and helped empower us to teach differently. Here, we share three of their stories in order to remind all of us why we teach and why we need schools that work for all students, not just those who arrive primed to learn. As you read, think of your students and the difference you can make in their lives.

Meet Jade. In seventh grade, Jade had a heart of gold. In her binder, she stuffed childhood photos of herself and her dad. She loved hot chocolate and dying her hair. Some days she came to school with pink highlights; the next day, her hair would be blue. She wrote love poems to her boyfriend and sketched wedding dresses on her writing assignments. Jade lived in a group home for children. Her father started dating a new woman, and they decided they didn't want a child around, so they gave her up. Although two grade levels behind, Jade was a voracious reader of fantasy, a pleaser at her core, a girl who would always stay after class to push in chairs or share her sketches. But she was also often in trouble. In one instance, she ran away from school to try to visit her father. He called the police. The saddest part about the visit was that, when she broke into her old bedroom, the bed was gone.

Meet Roger. He was often seen in the same chair in the back of the classroom next to the window with his head in a book. He would rarely socialize with anyone, hated group work, and never raised his hand to participate. Having to do a project with craft materials or manipulatives sent him into a fit of frustration. Most of the time, he kept to himself and read. In fact, he read an entire college-level textbook in the first week of a summer class. He could process high-level, complex content that he would sometimes share one-on-one with a teacher. He thought he might want to be a neurosurgeon. Although Roger was labeled "gifted and talented" from an early age, he was failing four of his five classes by ninth grade, was severely depressed, and was at risk of dropping out of school. He did not understand the subtle nuances of communication needed to interact with his peers. On the other hand, he did not have to be told what to read and when. He had no desire to complete the inane worksheets he was given for homework that were just about rote skills he had already mastered. He left entire assignments and tests blank. He had lost patience with how bored and out of place he felt in school.

Meet Axzavyeir. He was brought to residential foster care after his parents' rights were terminated when he was eleven. He was angry and distrustful of adults and "the system." He could barely read or write, was often violent toward peers and staff, and had a hard time being respectfully compliant to authority if he felt he was not respected. But Axzavyeir wasn't a difficult student, he was a reluctant student with complex behavioral issues that were magnified by his past trauma. Axzavyier was violent because he had experienced deprivation of essential resources (food, shelter, clothing, safety) at an extreme level from a very young age. In his world there was only one way to get what you needed to survive or to protect what you had, and that was violence. Axzavyeir never went beyond what he felt was necessary to keep himself safe.

Axzayvier may not have been able to read a book or articulate his thoughts in the written format that traditional education emphasizes but he could read an environment, a person, or a group with clinical precision. And while he could be disrespectful, he could also be amazingly protective of those he did respect and would often try new things based on the suggestions of those trusted few.

We cannot imagine a system where these kids, all kids, are not able to get what they need to learn, to grow, to explore their own limits and push past them.

Before you continue reading, think for a moment about a student who has transformed you. Remember his or her name. What was amazing about that student and how did he/she change you? How does this student fit in with the variability of learning?

Jot down some notes, draw a picture or just write their name below. Take them on this journey with you.

We are all familiar with the experience of anticipating that one of our students was just not going to do well in our class no matter how much extra support we offered. We all know that sad lack of surprise when we hear that one, two, or three students have eventually dropped out of school. Were there decisions that could have been made differently? After our first couple of years teaching, classroom practice can almost become automatic: it's all too easy to keep going with the materials, resources, and routines that seem good enough. Indeed, so many of us teachers never feel we have adequate time or resources to make even the simplest changes to our curriculum or approach. We are trained to be equipped with backup strategies in anticipation of problems we know may arise. We work countless hours trying to reach all students—we have pull-out rooms for support, paraprofessionals to help in the classrooms, and individual education plans. We work nonstop during the day to try to help each and every student. Nonetheless, we still are losing some of our students.

For us, UDL offers a framework to reach and engage all students. In our classrooms it might feel satisfying to have every student working on the same math problem at the same time. It can feel empowering to deliver an engaging lecture to a group of students. But if these practices do not align with what we currently know about variability and learning, if they are not meeting the needs of all students, are they the best design? What would it mean to trade them for new ways of teaching? We are not saying that these practices have to go, but the design of the experience needs to be fundamentally shifted.

Know Your Goals

There is nothing worse than getting in the car for a road trip with no idea of your destination, thinking: Where are we going? How long will it take? Do we need to pack, get snacks, and download movies? Are we bringing the dog? When we do know where we are going, we can anticipate what we may need to help us get there. This can alleviate worries or concerns and help us be strategic about how we prepare. We can anticipate where there may be roadblocks or barriers.

In our process of unlearning, once we understand that a UDL "learning buffet" can help our classroom context support the variability of our students, we can begin to take the critical concrete step to design that buffet by first clarifying the goal or purpose of the learning experience. Focusing on goals is so essential for UDL implementation, and it can take time and collaboration to really break down the standards, skills, social-emotional skills, behavioral expectations, and practices we want for our students. But before we get to the concrete strategies to do this (we promise this is coming), we first need to reflect on the current goal-setting systems that are in place.

Take a critical look at how we currently set goals for our lessons. Regardless of your role—whether as an administrator thinking about the vision and mission of the school or as a classroom teacher preparing for a lesson tomorrow or a coach preparing for a one-on-one meeting with a parent—how do you currently set and share goals? For UDL, it is essential to really clarify the goal, or central purpose, of the learning experience. When we focus on the goals, then we can then identify the roadblocks or challenges that may prevent students from achieving those goals. We know whether and how we can be flexible when we are crystal clear about the goal for that part of the lesson. Note that in this book we use the word "goal" to describe the intended learning target for a lesson or unit, but you may use other terms, such as "objective," or "students will be able to (SWBAT)," or some other phrase.

If we are driving to a local coffee shop from our home, we will plan differently than if we are driving to a coffee shop in another state. When we know the destination, we know whether we might want to walk, take the bus, or drive. We can determine if we want the scenic or no toll route. We might have the directions listed step by step and have the voice read us each turn. We might use the bird's-eye map view and silence the voice. Depending on the destination, we choose from the GPS "buffet" of options for each trip we take. Depending on where we are starting from and what current preferences are, the options may also vary.

Imagine that the goal for a lesson you are about to teach is for students to solve a linear inequality. Reflect on what a "buffet" of options could be for students to achieve this goal. Why should they care (UDL Engagement Principle)? How can they build their understanding of how to solve this kind of problem (UDL Representation Principle)? What options are there for them to show their understanding of solving these problems (UDL Action and Expression Principle)? Notice that if the goal for the lesson changes—say, if the goal is for students to work as a team to solve a linear inequality problem—then the "learning buffet" of options changes to include flexible ways students can engage in the group work (for example, there could be options to see effective examples of group work or to self-reflect on their contributions).

Roadblocks and Barriers

As you set off on your road trip, with the destination clear, we all know it is not usually a smooth and easy ride to get there. There will be traffic jams, detours, spans of open road that will seem to take forever, and you might even be sitting next to someone who gets carsick in the hilly parts. Some of these roadblocks along the way can be avoided. However, some of the challenges we encounter will be ones we need to confront and learn how to handle. With our destination in mind, how might we be able to better plan ahead to anticipate barriers or to avoid unnecessary obstacles and frustrations?

It is important that we break down our goals into subcomponent parts so that for each part of the journey we know exactly where we are trying to go. This helps us see the options that might be most pertinent for each part of the trip. And we do not need to do this alone. In our classrooms, we need to share expectations with students, so they can prepare what they need for their learning journey. For example, you may write the goal on the board, post it on assessments, or discuss it to make sure everyone understands the purpose, relevance, and steps necessary to achieve it. We will unpack this process in more detail in Chapter 6, but if you are planning a lesson with a clear goal (whether for a short part of a lesson, for the full lesson, for the unit, or for the overarching year in your class), then share this goal with learners and together anticipate barriers.

Once you identify the main barriers or challenges in the lesson, you can brainstorm options that could help reduce some of these roadblocks. Sometimes we may decide that productive struggle for students is important in itself and they may not need too many options. Other times, we may want a more bountiful buffet of learning options. When the goal is clearly modeled and shared with students, then we can work together with them to anticipate obstacles in the learning and design a "buffet" enabling each student to reach the destination.

Goals + UDL Guidelines = A Powerful Design Combination

Once you embrace variability and focus on goal-setting, it's time to be intentional about the different pathways that are possible to reach the goal. On a road trip across the country, you may choose to drive straight through on your own, hardly stopping for gas. Others may want to play song lists with friends and stop to snap a picture every time they cross a state line. There may be some required stops: we will need to get gas and food. If the goal is to get across the country, there's no "easy" way to get there, as we will all reach the same destination.

What if Universal Design for Learning is the framework that will guide the redesign of learning environments to transform our classrooms so we are able to reach all of our students in goal-driven learning that is personalized to their needs? What would it look and feel like to have classrooms full of engaged students tackling rigorous course material because they understand *why* learning is so critical and they know that they have the options to challenge themselves and get support as necessary? With every goal you craft, ask yourself and ask students: Why does this matter? How is this relevant? What does success look like?

Imagine that students need to write an argumentative essay that smoking should be banned in public spaces. Without knowing the students in this classroom, we can already anticipate variability using the three UDL principles. There will be variability in Engagement: some students will not be interested, will not put forth effort, or will not think they can accomplish this task well. Others will be interested in the topic and ready to go. There will be variability in Representation: some will not have any background about smoking in public spaces and some will not know what should be included in an argumentative essay. Others may have written dozens of argumentative essays and have strong writing backgrounds. There will be variability in Action and Expression: some will not know how to start writing, how to express their thoughts clearly, or will not be able to plan their essay. Others will know just what kind of graphic organizer can help them get started and have a thesis crafted effortlessly. Using the UDL Guidelines, we can anticipate the learner variability and some of the barriers our students are likely to face.

Clear goals make it evident when a resource or tool can be used to support the learning and when it cannot. If the goal of a lesson is for students to understand the quadratic equation, a calculator and a worked model example may be used to help scaffold the calculations so students can hold in mind the other steps they are focusing on to learn the quadratic equation. If the goal of a lesson is to learn computation, the calculator should probably not be used. Clear goals make it possible to align your rubrics and assessments so you are sure you are measuring the intended goal. When we have well-crafted goals, students can determine if and how they are making progress to achieve them.

In classrooms where UDL is implemented, one of the big changes is that goals become a critical part of the conversation. Teachers break down standards and all the different subcomponents of a lesson and highlight goals more thoroughly. Students are more involved in developing their own learning goals. In addition, the UDL Guidelines are used by both the teacher and students to help select options that will deepen the learning. The UDL Guidelines provide a road map to reflect on how to infuse additional options into a lesson that support the goal and reduce unnecessary barriers. Students start to develop a deeper understanding about how different options can help their learning. The "learning buffet" becomes intentional and proactive. The context is designed to support the anticipated variability of the students, and that engages more students.

Think of the options as scaffolds for student learning that ultimately are intended to be removed over time, like the scaffolding on the side of a building. Once students better understand the quadratic equation, the calculator and model example will not be as necessary. As students choose to use the different options, they learn more about their own learning needs and what helps them make progress toward the goal.

Continue Your Unlearning Cycle

The second stage of the Unlearning Cycle is about thoughtful and intentional goal-setting. This understanding leads to the purposeful and intentional use of flexible options in your lessons to reduce unnecessary barriers.

A common misconception at this point in learning about UDL is that we just need to offer lots of options or that we need to use every one of the UDL Guidelines in a lesson. However, that is not UDL, and this misconception often frustrates teachers, as we simply do not have time to offer countless options for our lessons and it can seem overwhelming to assess for all of the options students might use. In addition, there is often the concern at this point that students will be overwhelmed by too many choices. At this stage of UDL implementation it is common for us to hear:

- "I offered lots of options, but students hated all the choice."
- "I was exhausted trying to assess all the different ways students turned in their work."
- "I don't have time to offer that many options in all of my lessons."

This is where goal-setting is so critical for UDL implementation. Making the goal specific and relevant and aligning the assessments and rubrics to the goal requires time. Take it one step at a time. Working with students to include options for Engagement, Representation, and Action and Expression that align with the learning goal is indeed time-consuming. But these are the elements critical to transforming our learning environments to support learner variability and to support learners in rigorous learning opportunities. You will never stop deeply analyzing your goals; and with UDL, we will constantly revisit and reflect on the goals. In Chapter 6, we have strategies to work with you to develop your goals, as intentional goal-setting is a critical tipping point for UDL implementation.

Where Are You Now?
Questions for Reflection:

- How do you set and share goals with your students?
- Why should they care about those goals? How are they meaningful or relevant?
- What "buffet" of options will they have to help them progress toward those goals? Are there options for Engagement, Representation, and Action and Expression?
- How will students know if they have reached the goals or how to monitor their own progress along the way?

What resonates so far with UDL? What questions do you still have? Jot them down and we hope to answer them in this book or reach out to us to begin a conversation.

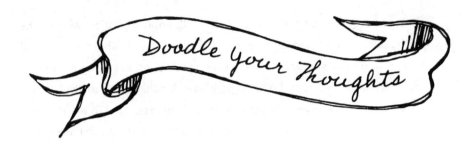

3 Transform Your Tried-and-True Techniques

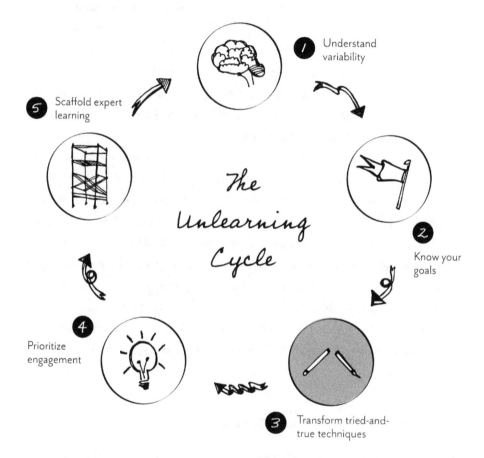

1 Understand variability

5 Scaffold expert learning

The Unlearning Cycle

2 Know your goals

4 Prioritize engagement

3 Transform tried-and-true techniques

Break Those Habits

Do you bite your nails or crack your knuckles? Brush your teeth at the same time and in the same way each day? Always sit in the same seat in a faculty meeting or at the lunch table? Take the same route home through your neighborhood?

Habits are really important, as they allow us to manage routine, everyday experiences without exerting too much cognitive energy. We make a cup of coffee, go for a walk, take out our notebooks when we get into a class, or whatever the routine action may be. We don't have to think about how we brush our teeth because we have been doing it for so many years in roughly the same way—and this is a good thing in terms of our cognitive capacity. Habits help us develop shortcuts that save us time and energy.

Habits typically are synced with a cue or trigger from our environment (it's right before bedtime) and a series of actions (we apply toothpaste and brush our teeth). And habits are also associated with a reward: your brain or body, or both, enjoys something that the habit offers (clean teeth and fresh breath). If there comes a time when you need to try to brush your teeth differently—perhaps you have braces or need to watch your gumline—it takes more energy to focus on and control the new actions in order to break the automatic routine. When someone sits in "your" seat at a meeting, it can be a flummoxing moment.

In the brain, many systems are involved in habit formation. The prefrontal cortex is involved in making decisions and directing goal-directed behavior. Motor cortex coordinates actions in combination with the cerebellum, emotion centers are activated, and memory centers are then called upon to encode the learning. Actually, habits don't require that we learn anything new. And when habits become automatic, the basal ganglia area of the brain takes over and the frontal lobe actually goes more or less offline. This is actually a little surprising when you think about it: when something becomes a habit, the part of our brain that makes goal-driven decisions is no longer as active! With habits, the brain starts working more automatically, using less energy, and starts to "do these complex tasks without really thinking about it" (Duhigg, 2012).

Our Habits in the Classroom

What are the habits we have integrated into our classrooms? How do these influence the habits or generalizations our students develop about their learning in our classrooms or schools? While some may be good and effective, others may be antiquated, or perpetuate inequities, or actually be harmful.

Habits rely on cues from the environment. Smokers may find that after lunch or on their walk home, they get the craving to smoke, as they are surrounded by sights, smells, or sounds that are familiar to their habits. We may find that, as a teacher, as soon as we stand in front of a class, we feel as though we need to deliver a mini-lecture. We need to read the book before we see the movie or videos. A student may find that, once in a history class, his or her body language assumes a negative, deflated attitude that is not present in other situations. These habits are often unconscious; we fall into them without even being aware. We may also not be aware of the subtle cues from our environment that can trigger them.

This is where UDL has a powerful potential for impact. UDL requires that we set rigorous goals and provide flexible options for all learners to achieve the goals. It is through access to flexible means that students have the opportunity to try something new, to break from their ineffective habits, or to take charge of their own learning pathway. Sometimes a small change can have a profound impact on learning and engagement. We can make our general education classrooms places where all students are able to learn flexibly and participate. But how can we change some of our teaching habits that may get in the way?

When the usual cues and rewards are not present, it is more likely we can change a bad habit: smokers may be more likely to shift to a new pattern if they are in a new location. In fact, Duhigg (2012) suggests that to break a habit, it's best to take a vacation, because it changes the environment and therefore the context. Many of us have observed that, in a different context, our actions or our students' actions and behaviors can be dramatically different. A student who is terrified to deliver an oral presentation in science class may be the lead in a play. The tired, uninterested student becomes the life of the party when surrounded by his peers during after-school sports. Attitude and habits vary according to context. Context really matters.

As amazing as a good long vacation can be, we cannot simply send our students on unscheduled vacations. We also do not want students to be removed or not to include them. Our classrooms are better when everyone is included and all are valued for their variability. How can we transform teaching and learning habits that are not working so we reach and engage every student in the classroom?

Being Critical of Tried-and-True Techniques

Consider the following list of tried-and-true teaching techniques: ability grouping, teaching test taking, assigning homework, and reducing class sizes. Which of these do you use? What are some of your tried-and-true teaching techniques? Hattie provides examples of the false perceptions of what is tried and true in his book *Visible Learning* (2009). As an educator or administrator, you likely have an incredible toolbox of best practices, and when those best practices are not supported in research, it is tempting to brush off the research as fake news or alternate facts. Granted, you can probably find a single research study to support almost any practice, but when you're faced with a robust, meta-analysis, it warrants attention, contemplation, and transformation.

Visible Learning is one of the most impressive education research studies of all time as it analyzes the academic impact of 256 influences in 1,400 meta-analyses. The purpose of *Visible Learning* was to determine what really works when it comes to teaching and learning. The findings may surprise you because our beliefs sometimes differ from the reality of evidence-based practices. This is what Hattie refers to as the "grammar of schooling," the phenomenon wherein our long-term experience with schools and classrooms as students affects our beliefs about teaching (Hattie, 2009). The examples listed at the start of this section are part of this: ability grouping, teaching test taking, assigning homework, and reducing class sizes. Why, then, are these practices still occurring in schools? Why are so many teachers still assigning homework? Spending time helping students prepare for tests? Grouping students by ability, and advocating for smaller class sizes? These are million-dollar questions that require new answers so we don't stay entrapped in practices that have been proven to be ineffective or potentially harmful to our students.

Let us begin by looking at the research and evidence-based practices on the effects of homework. Recent research shows no correlation between homework and student achievement. It is important to examine why previous research argued the opposite, and why many teachers believe assigning homework is a valid way to increase student achievement. One of the most cited studies on the positive impact of homework on achievement was a meta-analysis conducted by Cooper, Robinson, and Patall (2006) although even in this study the authors cautioned, "the positive causal effect of homework on achievement has been tested and found only on measures of an immediate outcome, the unit test. Therefore, it is not possible to make claims on homework's causal effects on long term measures of achievement" (p. 53). Even with these findings, however, the meta-analysis has recently come under fire. Maltese, Tai, and Fan (2012) argue that the results of the Cooper et al. study are not valid, as none of the studies in the meta-analysis directly evaluated the amount of homework in each course and the attained grade in that course.

When Maltese and colleagues examined studies that measured the direct correlation between the time spent on homework and grades in a specific course, and accounted for differences in demographics, academic engagement, and prior academic achievement, they found no consistent relationship between homework and grades. The authors noted: "We entered this analysis believing that the completion of homework likely reinforced material covered during class time and that extra learning time with material would lead to higher grades and test scores for students completing it. However, our results indicate that, after controlling for relevant factors, completing any amount of homework is associated with no significant improvement to student grades" (p. 66).

When Katie was teaching, she admits that homework was a part of the routine. "I always was assigned homework as a kid and so I kept assigning it. When I really started to think about it though, the kids who finished the homework were the same ones who cared about their grades and excelled in class. My students who struggled in class were ones who didn't complete the homework. Well, what on earth was the point of that? Since I couldn't control what happened at home, I realized that their grades should really be based on mastery in class. It was a complete "aha!" moment, a discrepant event, for me. As I assigned less homework and focused more on optimizing the use of class time, engagement shifted. Work became about learning and not routine. I have to admit that I never got to a place as a teacher where I eliminated homework completely, but if I were to be back in the classroom, I'd be on my way there."

This is a strong example of how we believe that the apple is red even when there is no light and there is no color to be seen. UDL encourages us to examine our routines and methods and determine what our goal really is and how our design is supporting the intended outcome and the variability of our learners. If the purpose of assigning homework is to deepen understanding of a concept presented in class, but many in class don't yet have a basic level of understanding, what is the point? How can we transform a homework assignment in a way that aligns with the intended learning we hope to achieve?

As an example, in a ninth-grade English classroom, a teacher named Mr. Rodriguez wanted to encourage student collaboration through classroom discussions, a tried-and-true technique. He was frustrated that the same students always monopolized the conversation. He tried to use protocols that required all students to participate, but then the conversations seemed forced. He asked students to share the obstacles they felt they faced. One student noted that it was hard to think of something on the spot because she didn't have a lot of background knowledge on the topic. Another admitted that, as an introvert, she felt uncomfortable even participating in the discussions. As a result of this feedback, the teacher was able to pivot and make changes the next day.

At the beginning of the class, Mr. Rodriguez gave the students the option of reading an article or watching a short news clip before the conversation to activate background knowledge. Next, he offered two mechanisms for discussion: a fishbowl he would facilitate or an online Google chat (this group discussion technique is used in many companies).

The teacher also provided sentence stems and questions that would keep the conversations going in multiple ways. Every student participated and contributed to the discussion using one of the options. The chat transcript, especially, was pure gold! It provided an artifact for the discussion that could be accessed by all students and had the potential for students to review, to thematically code, or to share with students who may have been absent (and students who were absent could even participate!). Having the option to review the core concepts for discussion, summarize main points, and then share their own thoughts helped to optimize collaboration—either synchronously or asynchronously—and deepen the learning for more students.

Discussion Ideas

- (tech) Google Chat: Setting up a Google Chat or Hangout is easy and the chat can be accessed from any device—computer, tablet, or phone. Also there are options for direct messages as well as group chats so students can choose the group size that works best for them.
- (tech) #Slack: Educators can set up a classroom space where students can post comments, links, images, or articles for the class to see. Similar to Google, slack can be accessed from any device and students can have private or public discussions.
- (non-tech) Fishbowl: A small group of students has a conversation while others watch the discussion.
- (non-tech) Stump Your Partner: Students take a minute to create a challenging question based on the lecture/class content up to that point. Students pose the question to the person sitting next to them. To take this activity a step further, ask students to write down their questions and hand

them in. These questions can be used to create tests or exams. They can also be reviewed to gauge student understanding.

- (non-tech) Paraphrase Passport: A structure that requires each team member to correctly paraphrase or restate the idea of the teammate who spoke previously before being allowed to contribute his own idea.
- (non-tech) Constructive Controversy: Pairs in a group of four are assigned opposing sides of an issue. Each pair researches its assigned position, and the group discusses the issue with the goal of exposing as much information as possible about the subject. Pairs can then switch sides and continue the discussion.

Trade Up for New Ways of Practicing With UDL

After hearing about UDL for a while from his friend, an ice-skating coach wondered if UDL might help him address a challenge he was having in his skating lessons: he had mixed levels in a single class and he felt that his top skaters were bored (the coach assumed the misbehavior of his students meant they were bored) and his weaker skaters couldn't keep up. This coach decided to try to integrate UDL into one of his skating lessons. Here, he reflects on how this one group lesson became the discrepant event that ultimately transformed the way he conducted his skating lessons:

> I want all my students to learn in my skating lesson, of course, but I usually have 10–12 skaters of all different abilities in a very short session with limited space on the ice. It's challenging. Usually what I do is separate the students by their experience (old tried-and-true technique: labeling the skater). Then I give each group different activities to work on (old tried-and-true technique: differentiating based on the label). I skate around and give feedback. Often I give the same 6–7 comments to the students (old tried-and-true technique: teacher owning the instruction, timing, and feedback). This is how my skating lessons were given to me when I was learning to skate, it is what parents and students expect of the lessons, and it is how other coaches give their lessons.

I had heard about UDL but didn't think it could relate to me. Then one day I decided to try something different for one of my mixed group lessons. Focusing on the goal was very different for me. I set a clear goal for all of my skaters for this lesson: we were going to work on improving the lutz jump. I knew there would be variability in the skaters: some have a lot of background (UDL Guideline 3), execute the jump well (UDL Guideline 4), and are engaged and interested to put forth effort (UDL Guideline 8). To design my lesson to support this variability, I offered a few options that any skater could use as they worked toward the goal of improving their lutz jump. I made a video station where they could watch an expert lutz jump in slow motion, pause the video at different times, and use discussion prompts to highlight key techniques. There was the opportunity to practice the lutz jump (a single, double, or triple) and they could use my checklist of the six typical corrections that are needed for this jump with a partner to analyze and reflect on their jump. They could use their phones to video themselves doing the jump to analyze on their own jump with the prompt, or they could work with me.

It was a totally different experience. I was not repeating the same feedback dozens of times, my students were talking more with each other and asking me higher level questions. It was as though they were taking more ownership of the jump, instead of it being all about me giving them feedback. It was really amazing to watch.

UDL fundamentally switched the way the entire skating lesson was conducted. It allowed for some of the old, frustrating patterns and habits to be broken, and as a result more rigorous and engaging learning was able to take place. UDL shifted the focus of the experience to be on proactive design of the learning environment up front to support the anticipated variability, in service of the goal, and with an outcome that engaged more skaters. Options for Engagement (such as collaboration, feedback, and authentic examples), Representation (such as the video, watching each other, and highlighting key components of the jump), and Action and Expression (such as the checklist and opportunity to practice and evaluate) invited more skaters into the lesson, engaging them in richer ways, with better outcomes. For this coach, trying a lesson in a new way and seeing the difference in level of participation and action from students provided the discrepant event that was meaningful and relevant for both him and his students. It helped him shift some of his practices and engaged him to continue trying UDL.

Take a look at the UDL-aligned beliefs about learning in Table 3.1. Reflect on the importance of each for your teaching and lesson design. There is also a space to add some of your own essential beliefs about teaching and learning. Identify specific actions you take in your classroom to design for your teaching and learning beliefs. Which tried-and-true techniques do you use that may not align with these beliefs? Which techniques are really effective?

Table 3.1.

Essential UDL-Aligned Belief About Learning	Is This an Important Belief for Your Teaching?	What Techniques Do You Integrate Into Your Classroom to Support This Belief?
I believe every individual can learn.		For example, I communicate high expectations to each student.
I believe there is variability among students in every situation.		I provide more than one way for students to take part in a lesson.
I believe the design of the environment makes a difference in how learners can succeed (or fail) so I work to change the environment, not "fix" the student.		I have flexible spaces in my classroom for students to work as they need.
I believe each individual will vary in each different situation (context matters).		I do not tell students what they need. I ask them what will help them.
I believe learners have jagged learning profiles of strengths and weaknesses, not innate learning styles.		I use the language of variability.
I believe how we set expectations influences learner outcomes.		I let students set some of their own goals.
I believe all learners can benefit from flexible learning pathways.		Any student can use any option in the lesson.
Add your additional ideas of core learning beliefs:		

As an example, when you believe that every individual can learn, you likely have a number of strategies that optimize the outcome of every student in your classroom. You may, for example, allow all students to revise work when they didn't meet or exceed expectations, but you acknowledge that not all students learn at the same pace and some may need additional feedback and opportunities to learn. If you believe that there is variability among students but provide only one way for students to participate in class, then you might consider adding some more flexibility for students to participate in class.

In order to start to make subtle shifts in our practices, we need to break some of our old teaching habits and trade them for some new ones that support the beliefs we have about student learning. These three steps can provide guidance for how to change old habits and routines (Bonchek, 2016):

1. **Recognize that the old model is no longer relevant or effective.** Reflect on the parts of your lesson or classroom or school that are not working for all students. Ask yourself whether everyone is learning and succeeding with our current model, methods, and techniques.

   - Who is *not* learning and what do we currently do about it?
   - What is not working in my classroom or school that I want to change?

   By answering these questions honestly, you take the first step to unlearning an entrenched teaching habit that poses a barrier for student learning.

2. **Find a new model that serves your goals.** Models serve as representations of larger, more complex processes. They break down a complicated, multifaceted process into simpler terms. The UDL Guidelines offer a model for aligning our teaching practices with what we know about the variability of the learning brain. It provides us a way to intentionally reduce barriers in planning lessons by changing the environment—not by labeling or modifying or removing a student from the classroom. If you have another model that serves the goal of designing instruction for all learners, then go with that. If not, you might want to give UDL a try.

3. **Ingrain new mental habits.** Note that you will be tempted to fall back on old ways of thinking and doing. Relying on these routines saves us cognitive energy! Change is not linear or simple; it is complex and requires work and effort. Do not change everything all at once. Instead, explore the new knowledge by trying one thing out and exploring how it works. For example, in the Unlearning Cycle, we recommend clarifying your goals. Then, choose one or two items to change

or to add to the "learning buffet." For example, you could first start to make some changes to the classroom environment: maybe not all students need to sit at their desks, but there could be standing options, rockers, floor space, or beanbags (yes, even in high schools and college classrooms!). Maybe you focus first on the UDL Representation Guideline: Provide Options for Perception to try to customize the display of information, or have an option for your auditory and visual information. Maybe you turn on captions for a video, or record key ideas from a verbal discussion on the whiteboard. See what happens when you provide a digital handout that can be customized. Start with your goal and try using just one UDL Guideline. This can help you build a new "UDL" mental habit for how you design your lessons.

Allison used this three-step process to think about the old model for teaching that was not quite working for her. She then used goals and one of the UDL Guidelines to begin to develop a UDL-aligned mental habit of mind.

1. **The old model that didn't quite work:** When she was first teaching, Allison appreciated Howard Gardner's multiple intelligences (MI). This framework challenged the traditional notion of one intelligence, or IQ. However, she had colleagues who would hand out MI sheets for students to identify the intelligence that best fit them. They created stations for "bodily kinesthetic" students or "linguistic" students. While the MI model resonated, it didn't fully work for her, and she never felt comfortable giving herself or her students a label. The list of intelligences did not quite seem to capture the complexity and variability she had experienced as a learner and as a teacher.

2. **The new model that served her goals:** The UDL model of variability and context better fit her experience and understanding of learning. Understanding how the context can influence the preference was incredibly important for her: in one environment, a student may prefer a linguistic option, and in another she may prefer a kinesthetic. Having a more flexible context, or "learning buffet" would help students make strategic choices. This was a powerful "aha!" moment for her.

3. **Ingrain new mental habits:** She started to deliberately use the language of variability. Instead of saying "This student is a visual learner," she would instead say, "There will be variability in how students want to perceive this information." Instead of saying "gifted student" she would instead say, "There will be variability in background understanding or in performance of this topic."

Now it's your turn. Take a moment and think about your pre-UDL model. If you're new to UDL, start by describing what you use in your current teaching and lesson planning model. Identify some of the habits and routines you use. Use our stories, anecdotes, or Table 3.2 to reflect on your teaching techniques. We hope this will help you start to transform some of the tried-and-true practices that do not quite resonate with your core values and beliefs about teaching and learning or that do not work well for student learning.

Table 3.2.

Your Turn! Shifting Your Tried-and-True Techniques
Pre-UDL model (This can be your current model of teaching). Jot down what works and what does not really work:
Model that aligns with your goals and beliefs about student learning (such as UDL):
Ingrain new mental habits (just focus on one or two concrete action items to start):

Continue Your Unlearning Cycle

The third stage of the Unlearning Cycle is about identifying tried-and-true techniques that may not work and breaking those habits. So much of our practice has been influenced by our own experiences in classrooms and can be set in old routines that may or may not be grounded in the best practice. It takes deliberate effort to step back, reflect on which practices are truly most effective for our students and for our learning goals. This understanding provides the rationale for why it is necessary to shift some of our classroom routines and habits. We hope the steps of the Unlearning Cycle will help you in this. Focus on variability, the context, or goal-setting as first steps. At this point, we hear comments such as:

- "I have used that technique since I started teaching, of course it works—well, it may not work for everyone."
- "When I knew the goal, I tried one new option for students to choose and for the first time, this one student worked harder than I had ever seen before."
- "UDL helped me better understand why something was working (or was not working)."

UDL understanding starts with our fundamental assumption that all learners can learn and that their capacity to do so can be influenced through the design of our learning environments. But UDL evolves to a more complex way of thinking and intentionality of design for learning that shifts our mindset and practices in order to meet the needs of all students. Moments of student "ahas!" in learning or engagement in a task can be powerful moments that inspire us to continue to refine and change our own practice. The ultimate goal is a design for learning that supports every individual, encompassing the broadest range of learner variability in our classrooms.

Where Are You Now?
Questions for Reflection:

- What professional practices, habits, or ways of thinking have not quite resonated for you in your teaching or learning?
- How does the Unlearning Cycle up to this point (understanding variability, knowing your goals, and transforming your tried-and-true techniques) support you in being intentional about the goal-driven learning buffet that is available in your classroom?

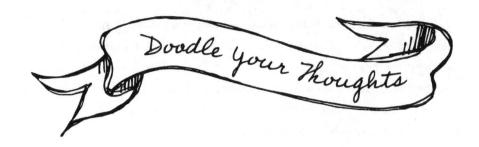

Doodle Your Thoughts

4 Prioritize Engagement

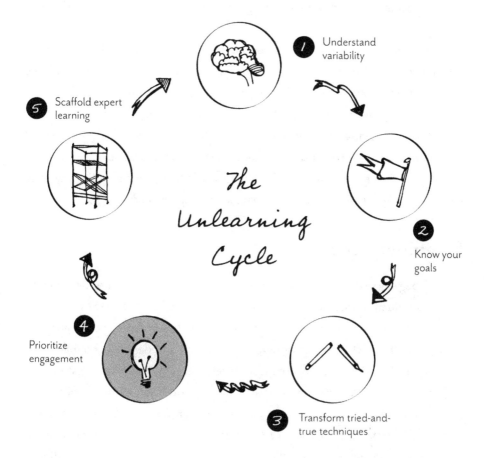

The Unlearning Cycle

1. Understand variability
2. Know your goals
3. Transform tried-and-true techniques
4. Prioritize engagement
5. Scaffold expert learning

The Damn Segway

Have you ever tried to ride a Segway? As you may know, a Segway turns differently from a car: to turn right or left, you move a small knob forward or backward with your right hand.

Allison went on a Segway tour of Washington, DC, and it was a total disaster. "I kept wanting to drive it like a car, where turning to the right meant going right.

I had to keep reminding myself, 'forward twist turns right!' Plus, if I leaned even the slightest bit forward, the Segway accelerated forward—and I kept leaning forward!"

Unlearning old driving habits became especially challenging when the group started trying to navigate the streets of D.C. with pedestrians, cars, and sights to see. Imagine crossing a crosswalk, seeing the countdown of seconds left to make the cross safely, and being unable to get the damn Segway to move. It's panic time.

Allison recalls, "I only crashed a few times. Once the teacher saved me before I plummeted head-on into a tree—and the whole experience became even more comical at night when my lone headlight could be seen from a distance rocking forward and backward as I struggled to keep up with the group."

Let's just say Allison did not make it through the full tour, and the guide seemed relieved when she shared her intent to call it a night. How could she have unlearned her years of driving more successfully? She has not been back on a Segway since then—what might it take for her to reengage in that experience?

Cognitive Load

Allison's Segway story bears some resemblance to the classroom. For some students, there is so much to focus on in a classroom that it can be hard to know where to direct their cognitive energy. A lesson may require an understanding of language or background that is challenging, or new skills to which a student may not have even been exposed. And this can absorb most of their energy and focus and destroy their engagement in the task. We often embed so many additional required skills in our lessons; for example, students must participate in group work, be organized and write neatly, do the reading, use only a blue pen, and more! Sometimes our content and directions are only given verbally, so students must hold all of the information in mind as they start into an activity.

Underlying all of our cognitive tasks are emotions. When emotions are drained, so is the ability to learn. Think of your brain as a vessel that can be emptied or filled with water: it fills up when you have to focus your attention or do something, when you are feeling intense emotions, or when there is a lot going on in the environment. Also note that "environment" includes not just the external environment but also stimuli from your own body and your own thoughts and emotions. For instance, if

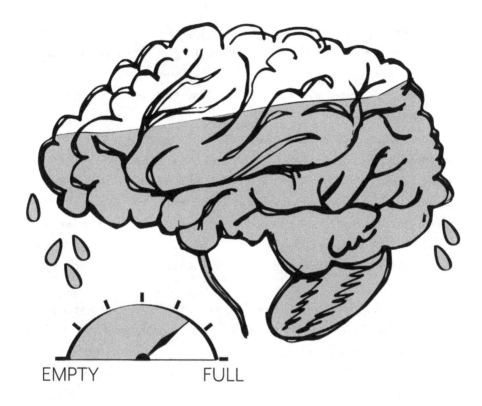

EMPTY   FULL

you are reading this chapter in a busy environment or with a side conversation going on nearby, or if you are feeling nervous about something that is coming up later today, you are likely not paying very close attention to the text as you read because your brain is already filled. "Cognitive load" is a way to describe the necessary effort it can take to complete a task. When cognitive load is tapped, it can decrease task completion and reduce flexibility.

Support Cognitive Load Through Engagement

One of the most common questions we hear about teaching is "How do we get a student who does not want to 'pick up the fork' (from the buffet analogy) to pick up the fork and start eating?" How do we engage students—all students—in learning? UDL offers a framework for approaching this challenge.

In a lesson, we know there will be variability in how students feel equipped to take on a task. When they perceive that the material is relevant or authentic to them, that they are safe and comfortable in the environment, and that there are resources to help them get the job done, then they may be more likely to be able to take the steps they need to achieve the goal. When we integrate the UDL Guidelines into our lessons, we support emotions necessary for learning by providing flexible options that help students gain access to resources that support the demands of the task.

Often simple solutions can fundamentally shift students' perception of a task and influence their engagement in the learning. For example, when a teacher let a student listen to a recording of the reading, that student could go at her own pace and pause and rewind when she needed to. She demonstrated much deeper engagement in the reading and participated more in the discussion than when the teacher had read the passage aloud to the entire class. This goal-driven, UDL-aligned strategy supported the student's engagement for learning and reduced the cognitive load.

We can look at the UDL Guidelines as a tool to help reduce our own cognitive load for how we design lessons. Providing options for Representation can help students build the necessary comprehension, so they are more ready to take on more challenging learning. Providing options for Action and Expression enables students to take physical action and express or communicate their understanding. They can monitor their progress toward the goal. In the next section, we will focus specifically on the engagement guidelines. It might seem straightforward to recognize how a graphic organizer or supplying background knowledge can support cognitive load, but how is engagement also doing this?

Engagement strategies often cited by teachers include having a "hook" at the start of the lesson, a game to play, or a point-reward system. But UDL challenges us to think more profoundly about engagement. UDL does not define engagement by a fun meter but by how we design to recruit student interest, foster sustained effort and persistence, and support self-regulation. When thinking about the engagement of your lesson using the UDL lens, ask yourself the following questions:

- How do we find relevant and authentic examples, ways for students to make choices, and options to minimize potential threats and distractions?
- How do we invite students to make the goals salient, vary the resources and demands for a task, foster collaboration, and provide process-based feedback?

- How do we promote expectations for all of our students, facilitate personal coping skills, and develop self-reflection as an important learning skill?

A physics teacher, Ms. Sheffield, shared her frustration about student engagement: her students tended to do the regular problems fairly well but usually did not make it through the higher-level challenges. And the latter tend to be the more applied, real-world skills for thinking like a physicist. To approach this problem of engagement using UDL, instead of providing more practice problems [her tried-and-true technique from previous years], she turned to the UDL Engagement guidelines. She thought about how she could make those challenging problems more relevant to students, and she set a "learning buffet" to reduce barriers.

Her ideas included having "getting started" prompts to help students see how to start a problem. She offered them the option to work with partners (or not) or with her in a guided session. Finally, she recorded video options to show how to solve a similar kind of problem. At the end of class, she used her exit ticket not just to assess content understanding but added a question about how they had sustained their effort and persistence by using different strategies when they felt stuck. As a result, she saw more students try and successfully engage with these higher-level problems. She also found that the quality of discussion about these problems was much richer than it had been in previous years. Notice how the UDL Guidelines supported deep engagement in learning.

We can anticipate that our students will always vary in their engagement with the material. What fires up and is interesting to one student will bore or overwhelm another. When we provide options to make authentic connections with students and their cultures and use relevant real-world examples, we are engaging with students in a way that can activate emotions for learning. Some students will bring extreme trauma, anxiety, or stress to school with them. Others will wrestle with self-regulation and motivation. This is where flexible options for learning are most critical. These reduce cognitive load and provide more equitable opportunities. In designing flexible opportunities for students to take breaks when they need to, to move around if that helps them, or to keep pushing when they are engaged in a powerful moment in their learning, we support more students in the challenges of learning. These strategies may seem simple, but they can be critical for us to address if we are to truly design for the variability of student engagement.

Teacher's Engagement With UDL Implementation

Some of you may now be saying, this is just too much! You took a look at the long list of UDL checkpoints and feel overwhelmed. We recognize how full and busy your days are, and that trying to integrate UDL can feel like too much because your cognitive load may be depleted. That being the case, it can feel overwhelming to plan additional options and choices because it takes more time. At first, that is true, because it does take time to make small changes in your daily routines, break habits, and try new ways of approaching lesson design.

Integrating UDL-inspired strategies and tools for enhanced engagement can take deliberate effort and may require intense focus at first. Yet the more familiar these simple shifts become, the less energy they will require— for both you and your students. Over time, you will adopt the UDL mindset of clarifying goals, designing options for predictable variability using the UDL Guidelines, and prioritizing engagement so you are able to incorporate UDL more effortlessly. It will become part of your new way of teaching and learning yourself. To have the cognitive energy to change our tried-and-true techniques we need to use the Unlearning Cycle to support teachers—and your engagement is critical.

Unlearning means taking a risk and trying something new. It means having an "aha!" moment of some kind wherein you experience discomfort and embrace it. It's the tipping point of conceptual change. Jon Mundorf—UDL pioneer and a teacher in a K-12 developmental research school at the University of Florida—calls it a "Wait, what?" moment. This tipping point is one of the hallmarks of true engagement, and it applies to us as teachers as well as to our students.

The Ugly Duckling had this experience when he finally saw his reflection in a pond and in a moment of clarity realized that he was beautiful—"Wait, what? That's me?" It's the moment of regret when the princess looks longingly at the frog as he changes into a prince and knows that she doesn't have a chance because of her black heart. "Wait, what? I could have kissed a prince?" It's the moment when you're confident that you have been using best practices and meeting the needs of all of your students and then you learn about Universal Design for Learning for the first time and you realize that creativity will only take you so far and you have to unlearn everything before you can truly learn about UDL.

This moment can feel uncomfortable, as though we are letting go of our sense of structure and of who we are as educators. And yet, that feeling of discomfort is a sign that there is more to learn, that there is purpose, that we have to tread a path that we weren't sure even existed. We want our students to recognize and embrace that feeling, and in order to do that, we have to embrace it ourselves.

Share Moments of Wonder

No matter how entrenched our habits and routines may be, our brains are pliable and we can change them in surprisingly short amounts of time. Even adult brains gain hundreds of new neurons in the hippocampus every day! Every brain can change. Yes, some changes may feel uncomfortable at first, but that's why it is so critical for us to work together, to focus on engagement, and to share what we are doing and trying in our classrooms and how it is impacting our students.

As we discussed earlier, discrepant events are moments that defy our expectations. They can surprise us or catch us off guard, as they have unexpected outcomes. We may wonder about these moments and want to try them ourselves: How many of you did the Diet Coke and Mentos experiment? Heard Yanny or Laurel? Saw the dress as gold-and-white or blue-and-black? The discrepant event challenges our years of experiences and expectations, and so even if we try to fall back on simple heuristics to explain it, we cannot. We can either oversimplify the situation or try to deepen our understanding about what happened (Longfield,

2009). We might think about what kind of discrepant event might help us "unsee" the apple as red even in complete darkness. We often wonder what kind of discrepant event might help educators "get" UDL without going through the Unlearning Cycle.

To be effective, discrepant events must be clear and obvious so that we recognize that our current way of thinking is dysfunctional. Because we hear Yanny as clear as day, we could assume it is impossible that someone else heard Laurel, or we can try to learn more. Discrepant events in our classrooms or schools can be powerful enough to encourage us to pause and reflect on what happened and to make changes in our actions. For example, a few educators described discrepant events occurring in their classrooms when they started implementing UDL that became powerful ways of engaging them to continue their learning:

- "Our PPI for students with disabilities went from 29 to 79 in three years while the state average went from 53 to 51." —K-12 assistant superintendent
- "We have had an 82 percent drop in suspensions this year. We have never seen this before." —Middle school principal
- "I had an 80 percent increase in students taking the practice tests, and not one student failed my course this year." —College professor

When these educators looked deeper to explain the discrepant events, moments that defied their expectations, the common thread among them was that UDL had been integrated into the design of the instruction. In each of these scenarios, the anticipated and expected outcomes did not align. For individuals who designed and witnessed these situations, these discrepant events changed their perception about how students were learning in their classrooms and rekindled the enthusiasm they had for teaching—and, in many cases, these educators started to become passionate advocates of UDL! They had experienced firsthand how the design of the learning experience could not just meet the needs and range of their students but lead to deeper engagement in learning. They saw how UDL could support them in transforming their lessons, and had no desire to go back to old ways of thinking or designing. Seeing the evidence of UDL in action inspired engagement, reflection, and further change. They even shared their exciting moments with colleagues, hoping they might inspire them to adopt UDL. However, because they had not gone through the

Unlearning Cycle, were likely resistant or still not ready to imbibe the UDL lemon juice.

When It Still Does Not Stick

You still might be worrying about this UDL framework. It's complex, takes time, and requires effort and energy (above and beyond the normal energy of teaching!). Perhaps you worry that students will make a bad learning choice or always take the "easy" choice if you offer options. You might be concerned that you will some lose control of the classroom if students are working in different ways, and this might leave you feeling uneasy about changing how you design the learning environment. In addition, you may not have the cognitive energy to try. After all, aren't most students basically okay? UDL may seem like too big a change. The risk may seem too high for the potential or unseen benefits in *your* classroom.

Discrepant events disrupt our routines by offering alternative outcomes to a "problem" we have because they do not lead to the expected, anticipated outcome. What if "that" student was able to be the star during a lesson? What if "that" student had insights that no one else had considered—and even you, the teacher, saw the problem in a new way that you hadn't thought of before! When students experience success and "aha!" moments of learning, it is one of the most engaging moments for that teacher. The best way to experience a discrepant event is not to hear about it secondhand but to experience it yourself!

Continue Your Unlearning Cycle

In this fourth stage of the Unlearning Cycle, you begin to really shift the design of your lessons and learning experiences. We recognize that it takes cognitive energy to make changes and it is too easy to fall back into old routines, but the engagement you will see in your students and that you will feel as an educator will be infectious! Classrooms at this stage can start to look and feel different, and you are likely to experience discrepant events that will motivate and make you want to continue to try one more thing in your classroom.

You may hear comments such as:

- "I think more now about why I am teaching this, is this the right goal, and why should students care."

- "I saw a student who had never written more than a page all year write over three pages today when he was able to choose his own comparative essay topic that interested him."
- "I know I can engage my students—it is not their problem, but the lesson design."

If educators have still not experienced their own UDL discrepant event at this point, you will likely continue to hear this comment: "I still want to see more examples of UDL in practice." This is a very common request. Every educator will need to go through the Unlearning Cycle at his or her own pace, and the most effective way to fully embrace UDL is to experience it in your own context. If you are a coach or administrator working to support UDL in your site, continue to provide flexible UDL options to model and share your journey.

Where Are You Now?
Questions for Reflection:

- What barriers do you face to engaging in UDL implementation?
- What is critical to motivating you to take first, small steps in your UDL implementation?
- What kind of discrepant event or "moment of wonder" can you share about your classroom that was a result of UDL implementation?

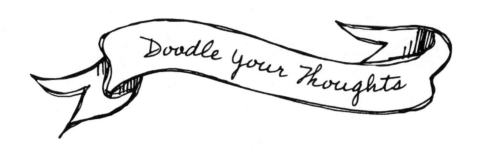

5 Relight the Pilot Light to Unleash Expert Learners

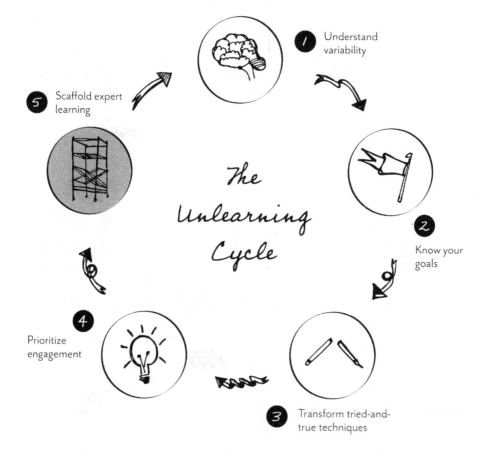

1. Understand variability
2. Know your goals
3. Transform tried-and-true techniques
4. Prioritize engagement
5. Scaffold expert learning

The Unlearning Cycle

Scene 1: Kids, each sitting on a stool, able to watch a chef making cookies—not all can see the chef. Barrier: Height of the counter. Not all kids can observe the baking process.

Scene 2: Kids at the counter, with the stools they need, watching the chef making the cookies. Barrier: All kids can observe the baking process, but they don't have the experience of making cookies.

Equality

Not everyone benefits from the same supports.

Equity

We can remove barriers by providing adequate supports based on variability.

Expert Learning

When we focus on individual needs, we not only promote equity, but also engagement and involvement.

Scene 3: Kids in different areas: a table, a counter, a workbench—all able to reach—not just see, enabling them to be more actively involved in the goal. With the goal to learn bake their own delicious cookie, they can make their own choices from the options in the environment.

Expert Bakers

Let's imagine that our classrooms are being represented by a baker with some baking apprentices. The goal in each sketch is that the bakers will be able to bake their own delicious batch of cookies that they will eat for a snack.

Now that you know the importance of goal-directed curriculum design, these sketches summarize a visual for UDL. The goal in each sketch is that the learners will be able to bake a delicious cookie they will eat for a snack. The first sketch represents equality: each participant is given a stool so they can take part in making cookies. However, as you can see, when given the same resources, only one child is able to observe the baking process. The middle sketch represents equity: each participant needs something different. In this scenario, different stools support different learners, offering them distinct modes for reaching and interacting with the "one-size-fits-all" cookie-baking activity. However, a barrier still exists: all the students can "see" but not necessarily participate in personalized ways that are meaningful and authentic to them.

In the third sketch, we shift our focus to reducing barriers in the design of the environment and thereby empower learners to use the tools they need to reach the goal. This is fostering the development of expert learners, who are purposeful and motivated, resourceful and knowledgeable, and strategic and goal-directed. In this image, the goal is to "make a delicious cookie." The bakers are given flexible stools and resources to use as they need to achieve this goal.

When examining the visual, let's consider how the UDL Guidelines help educators anticipate and address barriers through intentional design. As you go through this section, we are sure you will have additional suggestions. That is excellent. UDL strategies come to life in unique ways for each educator in each classroom and we invite and welcome this conversation.

For the Engagement Principle, we can again anticipate variability: some will be engaged, others not. We may need to think about how making cookies can be made more relevant to them (perhaps they could bring in one of their grandmother's cookie recipes) or how they can collaborate (some will want to work together, others may prefer to listen to headphones and work on their own). Some may want to work step by step with the head chef (teacher) or sample examples to help them understand what qualifies as a good cookie.

For the Representation Principle, we may reflect that some will already know how to bake, while others may have never picked up a spatula. Therefore, having options to watch a video of a baker making cookies, to provide the recipe, to have images that go along with the directions, or to demonstrate the baking process as is done on a cooking show can all help build relevant background. But not every baker needs to do each of these steps—they can choose what they need to best help them.

For the Action and Expression Principle, we can again anticipate variability. Some may have an arm cast or not be able to manipulate the dough. Some may need step-by-step directions to check off a list, while others may prefer to first try the baking techniques using a digital simulation (try cookie maker apps from Google or Apple). Each "baker," when truly given the option, may design this experience slightly differently, which is why UDL will never look the same in any two classrooms. Remember, the goal is critical. Notice how the design and decisions change when the goal changes.

This vision for education seems so straightforward: reduce the barrier that is preventing access to the goal and reflect on the higher-level, more meaningful purpose. Put the focus on the expert skill or content that we want all learners to achieve. The UDL Guidelines are our tool for doing so. The Unlearning Cycle will help us implement the changes we want.

The remarkable transition is that when we focus on removing the barriers, we stop labeling students and start opening the conversation that can lead to the discovery of other strategies or means to reduce the barriers. We foster community and collaboration to support learning and so we are all more willing to take risks.

With UDL, reaching every learner is not just about providing materials and fun activities, it is about offering intentional, flexible options so learners can discover new ways of engaging in the learning process. They become active, purposeful, and motivated. When curriculum builds in background and reinforces what students already know while working toward the clear, meaningful learning goal, learners are transformed. They become resourceful and knowledgeable, learning which materials and resources help them build the new background they need. Why should we

Remove & Reduce Barriers

Reduce the barrier that is preventing access to the goal and reflect on the higher level, more meaningful purpose.

Encourage Expert Learning

Put the focus on the expert skill or content that we want all learners to achieve.

Use Your Tools & Resources

The UDL Guidelines give you the tools to remove barriers & encourage expert learning.

The Unlearning Cycle will help us implement the changes we want.

settle for students who merely sit complacently on "the side of the counter" in our classrooms, complying with the task? We want all students to become more strategic and goal-directed in their pursuits.

Expert learning will vary in different disciplines. For example, an expert scientist will be different from an expert historian or musician; but the UDL Guidelines provide us with a common road map for providing access to engagement, background, and action that can extend across disciplines.

Why not strive to envision students who know how to access what they need to enrich their comprehension, to self-regulate through challenges, and to share and express what they know? UDL enables this transformative shift for learners. They not only learn how to set challenging goals for themselves and follow through, they also become lifelong expert learners.

Setting High Expectations

Sometimes the biggest barrier to achieving expert learning is our expectations—or the expectations students have of themselves. How many of us have heard from parents, students themselves, or our colleagues about what "this student can and cannot do."

The first study of teacher expectancy was published in *Pygmalion in the Classroom: Teacher Expectation and Pupils' Intellectual Development* (Rosenthal & Jacobson, 1968). Teachers were informed that certain students scored highly on the test that purportedly measured academic potential and would likely "bloom" intellectually during the year. Rosenthal and Jacobson hypothesized that teachers would have higher expectations for "bloomers," would behave differently toward them, and as a result those students' IQ scores would increase. The findings of the study supported the hypothesis. Students randomly selected to be "bloomers" gained significantly more IQ points than the students in the control group. This is such a powerful fact that we are going to say it again: the students chosen at random as expected to have academic gains were the ones who did!

The Pygmalion study describes how teachers' expectations of students can be such a powerful influence in the classroom. One experiment told teachers that the so-called weakest students were actually the strongest; and by the end of the school year these "weak" students indeed performed the most strongly. Our expectations and labels become self-fulfilling prophecies.

Where Are You Now?
Questions for Reflection:

This concept of teacher expectancy is so critical, we wanted to pause here for you to go back and reread this section or process it further.

- What are your expectations for each one of your learners?
- How do you think the UDL shift to firm goals and flexible means can reduce some of the expectancy effects that groupings and labels may imply?

So, why do expectations have so much impact? It has been suggested that the powerful effects of teacher expectancy result because students, consciously or unconsciously, adjust their performance to match teacher expectations (Al-Fadhli & Singh, 2006). This happens in three stages. First, teachers develop expectations for the future performance of students. Second, teachers treat students in ways consistent with those expectations. Third, this treatment influences students. Robert Merton (1948) coined the term "self-fulfilling prophecy" to explain the phenomenon when an inaccurate belief that something will happen actually causes it to occur.

Take gifted and talented programs, for example. It is not that we are not fans of gifted education, because we certainly are. We believe in a high quality of education for all students. However, gifted and talented education should not be reserved only for those students who show their potential early and in predictable academic ways. As lifetime educators, we have worked with thousands of students and tens of thousands of teachers. We know from these experiences that all people are capable of greatness. Every single student shows amazing glimpses of potential that we sometimes have to work hard to see but should never ignore. We feel the same way about teachers. They are comprised of a group of people so committed to the future of our nation that they chose a job that is often thankless, in which they are often underappreciated and overworked, and in which the entire world is critical of almost every decision they make.

Yet they persist and thrive far more when we believe in them, have high expectations for them, and give them the best of "gifted education" in their own professional development. What is good for gifted education is also good for every learner—the opportunity to access rigorous, personalized enrichment projects that meet individual needs. What we know from the Pygmalion studies is that all learners are gifted when we believe they are.

Reignite the Pilot Light

Imagine it's a weekend in the middle of a Massachusetts winter and your water heater quits. One second, you are hoping for a warm shower, and the next, you are boiling water on the stove to wash your hair. A friend clambers into your dirt crawl space under the house to investigate and comes back covered in cobwebs to declare, "Pilot's out—can't relight it." Not really a profound statement, but it sums up what sometimes happens in our classrooms. We enter our classrooms and students stare back at us. Some arrive ready to learn while others need us to ignite their love of learning. Sometimes, even when we try our hardest, students are not engaged in their education. Their pilot lights are out; but we can relight it.

We aren't born expert learners, we become them. Think about the term "runner." A lot of people call themselves runners. There are kids who run in road races, adults who celebrate after Couch-to-5k Races, marathon runners, marathon winners, and even ultramarathoners. Clearly there is a continuum of runners, and yet the skills they all possess and build upon require effort, persistence, and commitment to move further along the continuum.

Katie is the mom of four kids, and after she and her husband, Lon, competed in the Spartan Beast, the kids participated in a Spartan Race for kids. They ran through muddy corn fields, climbed rope structures, and jumped over hay bales. During Writer's Workshop in first grade, her son Brecan reminisced on the event when he penned a narrative that read: "First I was winning. Then I was losing. Then I was last." The last drawing of the narrative included him smiling with a medal around his neck.

After that race, Katie's kids said, "Mom, we are runners like you," and to some extent, that is true. They have all the resources they will need to compete someday in marathons if they choose. It's not that they have to be faster, or buy the best shoes, it's that they have to *want* to keep running, to find friends to run with, and to come back mentally from injuries like turned ankles, blisters, and shin splints. They have to be engaged enough to run when it's hot, when it's cold, and when it's raining. This is engagement, and believe us, it's not all fun, but the goal is clear and relevant and meaningful, and so runners persist.

The Novak kids will need to learn to be resourceful in order to learn about the best refueling strategies, the best warm-up and training techniques, and the best ways to rest. They also have to take action, and run, run, and run again until they can run farther and faster than they thought they could. In short, the Novak kids are all becoming expert runners.

As educators, we are challenged to teach and model for our students how to become experts at doing what they need to achieve their best learning: be self-directed, motivated, and goal-driven in their learning. Some days, this can feel incredibly challenging; but just like the heater, we can't allow our students to quit and we can't quit. We have to keep high expectations for all learners because our belief matters. We understand that our students face very real barriers that may prevent them from learning, but we are the ones who set the goals and expectations for learning in our classrooms. Let's design environments where every student is engaged, valued, and has autonomy around their learning. We can make this happen through our mindset and design. Let's not just settle for meeting the standards and test scores, but let's reflect on the expert skills, habits, and practices that we want every student to have for learning beyond our classrooms.

To do this, we have to collaborate with our students so their voices are at the forefront of design. This sometimes takes a leap of faith. After all, we were the ones educated as teachers and designers, not our students. When we were in school, our teachers designed lessons for us. We acknowledge that it may seem jarring to open up your planning process to students, but the belief that they have something to offer is evidence of our highest expectations for them. We want our students to become codesigners, not observers. To return to the cookie-baking analogy for a moment, we want our students to choose their recipes and experiment with cooking techniques, not merely watch us from stools at the counter.

The power of UDL really comes to life when we share it with our students so they can gain this language for learning and design that can be used throughout their education, as they enter college and the workforce, and as they develop their passions. Students can partner with us to co-construct high-level, challenging goals that are meaningful for them. They can help us design relevant options that they can use to meet their goals. In a society where most of the jobs of the future are ones that we do not even know about yet, building expert learning skills is critical if we want students to be able to adapt to succeed in new contexts. Expert learners know how to set goals and what they need to build their own unique pathways to achieve them.

For example, imagine an elementary school classroom where the goal is that all students write opinion pieces, supporting their point of view with reasons. A pre-UDL model may provide all students with the same prompt and an expectation that they demonstrate their understanding of the goal in the same format. A typical prompt may require students to give short speeches on their favorite food with the requirement for three reasons to support their opinion. But this goal allows for so much more than speeches about favorite foods. Honoring students as expert learners and having high expectations means saying: "Choose something you have a strong opinion about. It may be your favorite food, a club you want to create at the school, or something bigger like a country you would like to visit or a law you would like to pass. Take some time and make a list of things you have strong opinions about and choose one that you really want to share with the class." As a next step, you could ask them how they want to share their opinion. Some students could give a speech, while others may prefer to record a podcast, write a composition, or write a letter. There are so many possibilities when we share the responsibility for lesson design with our students.

Student Autonomy

Take a look at the images on the following page and reflect on how your classroom is structured. Where is the power centralized? Who is controlling the learning? How would you diagram your classroom?

The third image, which represents the concept of full autonomy for students, may seem daunting. Can you imagine telling a class of thirty first-graders to find their passion and learn everything they can to build expert learning about this passion without scaffolding? The educational outcomes could be chaotic, even disastrous!

UDL coach Bryan Dean worked with his students to reach a better understanding of how options he provided could better support their learning and how they could take more ownership in the design process. He thought about and worked with one student, but then took what he learned from this experience to share and make options available for all students. An innovative design for one learner can be valuable for all.

The student Bryan worked with, Walter, had an advanced understanding of mathematical concepts and an infectious passion for explaining these concepts. In Bryan's class, he and Walter worked together to design scaffolded learning options to

Not Inclusive
Some students are separated from general education classes

Groupings
Teacher assigns tasks based on levels or labels

Inclusive Classroom
Variability is valued in every individual

address some of his gaps in skill. They also thought about how to contribute to the class community by offering them similar tools and strategies, reteaching what they understood in a different way, or watching out for each other. Walter chose to help create lessons that were relevant to his fellow students and to reteach Bryan's lessons in a different way as he understood them. Walter was both a consumer and a producer, and the entire classroom benefited as a result. He was the epitome of an active, engaged, expert learner.

How can we begin to shape personalized opportunities that set students on a learning trajectory that ultimately fosters expert learning? This is where we recommend using the Unlearning Cycle to scaffold your design. Know the goals, anticipate variability, and reduce barriers using the UDL Guidelines to design a "learning buffet" of options for Engagement, Representation, and Action and Expression. Take a step at a time to transform your tried-and-true techniques so students are engaged and truly at the center of their own learning. Then reflect: Have you set high expectations for all students? Is there an opportunity for students to work with you to design the goals and options? How can we help students be autonomous agents of their own learning?

The presence of autonomy does not mean the absence of structure and continued rigor. Students may not yet have all the skills needed to accept the autonomy they are offered and may need a gradual release of skills and scaffolding in order to understand the nuances of each category. The first part of a school year may require more time for building such skills and establishing class routines for this new learning. Until our learners are expert learners, they will need options for feedback and guidance that scaffolding UDL can provide.

It is also important to note that not all of these varied types of options and the autonomy to make choices have to exist in every learning situation; it isn't even the goal that they all exist in a lesson or project. Let the goals drive the work. Anticipate variability. Focus on engagement. Engaging in a dialogue about learning is critical to building a community of expert learners.

Continue Your Unlearning Cycle

Typically at this stage, educators are becoming well-versed in UDL, setting goals, anticipating variability, and designing using the UDL Guidelines to focus on engagement and learning. Often at this stage of UDL implementation, students in that classroom begin to become more a part of the design of learning experiences— and may even use the language of UDL themselves in their work to help identify and remove barriers to their learning. They become more expert in their learning and are in control of setting their own goals and understanding which options help or challenge their work. You may hear students make comments such as:

- "I could really use an alternative representation of that information."
- "Can I show you how I know that in a different way?"
- "Here is where I got stuck and this is how I tried to get through that part."

In addition, at this point educators are feeling more confident in implementing UDL and have seen the impact it has had on their own classrooms. They hold high expectations for all their students and more fully understand how to anticipate variability and reduce barriers using UDL. At this stage, these educators often become UDL leaders or coaches in their own communities, as others want to find out more about what they are doing in their classrooms. You may hear comments such as:

- "UDL is like the 'umbrella' for my practice: it informs all that I do and aligns with the other initiatives that are in my school."
- "I think about UDL everywhere."

Ultimately, in the course of a UDL journey, UDL educators trade up for new ways of teaching and thinking about learning. They focus on how to scaffold and design for expert learning. UDL becomes a framework that supports other important initiatives and areas of focus. Over time and with continued reference to the UDL Guidelines, you will develop an even deeper appreciation of learner variability.

The goal of UDL implementation is not to "do" UDL itself but is to use UDL to reduce or eliminate barriers and to design for all students to become expert, empowered learners. It takes time and effort, but the impact on our students is worth it. We hope that through learning about this Unlearning Cycle, you feel more prepared and ready to start to take action in your classroom.

Where Are You Now?
Questions for Reflection:

- What helps you hold high expectations for all students?
- How can you use the Unlearning Cycle to design for students to become more autonomous in their learning?

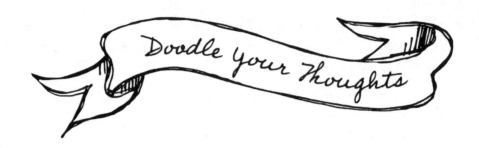

6 | Take Action

We asked you to reflect on one of your students to inspire you, to remind you why we are teaching and why we need to make sure that our design for learning supports every single student. In this book, we have guided you on your Unlearning Cycle to an understanding of why it is important to implement UDL and how the design can transform our classrooms. Each phase of the Unlearning Cycle requires deep introspection and self-reflection—and we hope we have offered opportunity for this. Now, in this chapter, we will provide activities and templates for taking action in order to implement UDL and change some of your teaching practices through the Unlearning Cycle. We encourage you to continue to keep your students in mind as collaborators in the process as you do so!

Understand Variability

Understanding that variability is the norm whereas "average" is as typical as a unicorn helps to explain why traditional models of teaching and learning do not meet the needs of our students.

Students have jagged learning profiles that can shift based on the context. As you implement UDL, it's important to be explicit with your students about what variability means, so that they recognize that they are complex and multifaceted—their skills and abilities cannot be reduced to a single label, but can shift over time or based on the supports or scaffolds available to them. Consider a student who may have been labeled as a "weak" reader unable to comprehend the central theme of a text. When given the chance to use text-to-speech for some assignments, this same student may be incredibly skilled at comprehending the central theme. The various tools, resources, and options we provide students at different times can shift their jagged learning profiles.

Here is an activity that will help you share the concept of variability with students so they can embrace their own jagged profiles and appreciate their own learning strengths and potentials. For different tasks, we want to encourage students to reflect about where they have strengths and weaknesses and how using different tools, resources, or strategies help them build on their strengths or shore up their weaknesses. We can reflect along with them about how their jagged learning profiles shift in different contexts. This will help them deepen their understanding of themselves as a learners and advocate for what they may need (or not need).

❋   ❋   ❋

Activity #1: For any lesson, identify some of the core skills and learning practices that are required. In our examples, we have used the UDL Guidelines as representing nine different dimensions of learning, but you can choose others that are important for your classroom. Then have students reflect on where their strengths and challenges lie. Brainstorm together how their challenges might be overcome by options in the environment.

Physical Science Classroom

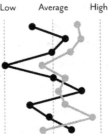

Student A

Low   Average   High

Interest
Persistence
Self-regulation
Perception
Language & Symbols
Comprehension
Physical Action
Communication
Executive Functions

Interest
Persistence
Self-regulation
Perception
Language & Symbols
Comprehension
Physical Action
Communication
Executive Functions

Student B

English Language Arts Classroom

Student A

Low   Average   High

Interest
Persistence
Self-regulation
Perception
Language & Symbols
Comprehension
Physical Action
Communication
Executive Functions

Interest
Persistence
Self-regulation
Perception
Language & Symbols
Comprehension
Physical Action
Communication
Executive Functions

Student B

Own the Guidelines

When variability seems overwhelming to plan for, look to the UDL Guidelines to think about the nine dimensions of learner variability. However, sometimes a barrier for educators when first learning about UDL is the language that is used in the guidelines. After all, they were written by researchers and do not necessarily reflect the language we would use in our classrooms with our students, parents, and colleagues.

Activity #2: Use Table 6.1 to rewrite the UDL Guidelines using language from your vocabulary that you can use with your students (see Novak, 2016 for examples). Collaborate with students to build language that aligns with the UDL Guidelines. In the table, language from the CAST UDL Guidelines site (Appendix B) has been included as an example to stimulate your ideas. For example, if you don't use the term "self-regulation," then rewrite this guideline in language more familiar to you and your students. Substitute your own terminology, perhaps something like, "I believe that I can get the job done." One of the incredible benefits of UDL is that it gives all educators and students a common language to use around learning.

Clarify Goals

Goals are nothing new in education, we have always incorporated goals or objectives and standards. However, UDL requires that we reframe and analyze our goals in a unique way. What exactly are students supposed to know, be able to do, and care about by being in this classroom? Why should students invest in this, and how is it meaningful for their communities? What are the educational goals, skills, practices, and habits of mind is this standard support?

We have discussed the importance of really analyzing goals to "de-tangle" the various components such as skills, content, behaviors, or social-emotional learning. When we tease apart these components of a goal and focus on how we intend to scaffold and support each one, we make it clear to students what success for each part looks like and how they can achieve it. Students attain higher levels of competency in each skill because they know what it is and what they need to do to achieve it.

Table 6.1.

UDL Guideline:	Your Own Terminology and Language
	Frame the UDL Guidelines using language you would use with your students or that has meaning for you.
Options to Recruit Interest *Spark excitement and curiosity for learning.*	
Options for persistence and motivation *Tackle challenges with focus and determination.*	
Options for self-regulation *Harness the power of emotions and motivation in learning.*	
Options for perception *Interact with flexible content that does not depend on a single sense like sight, hearing, movement, or touch.*	
Options for language and symbol *Communicate through languages that create a shared understanding.*	
Options for comprehension *Construct meaning and generate new understandings.*	
Options for physical action *Interact with accessible materials and tools.*	
Options for expression and communication *Compose and share ideas using tools that help attain learning goals.*	
Options for executive function *Develop and act on plans to make the most out of learning.*	

Activity #3: There are four main steps to "de-tangling" your goals, organized in Table 6.2:

1. Isolate all of the subcomponent parts of a lesson goal.
2. Determine which knowledge, skills, or contents are critical for students to learn for this part of the lesson.

Table 6.2.

De-Tangle Your Goal	Fifth-Grade Geography Teacher Example
Record your goal as you currently have it.	Original goal: Students will create a cereal box with their group that highlights the main accomplishments of an explorer. Then, they will present it to the class.
De-tangle the goal: identify and isolate all of the subcomponents:	To accomplish this, students will need to: • Do research to find the main accomplishments of the explorer • Organize their research and make meaning of it • Make a "creative and neat" cereal box that shows their learning • Work in groups • Present to the class
Clarify the primary goal for that part of the lesson.	New goal: Students will research the main accomplishments of an explorer. The teacher team decided the cereal box was not actually a skill they needed to focus on for this lesson. They also recognized that the group work and presentation was not essential for this part of this lesson.
Identify how there are tools or resources to support the critical parts of the goal.	Students could use the Internet and their textbook. The teacher team recognized that currently these were the only materials and resources available to support the research in this lesson. They brainstormed how they could create additional tools to help students be effective at honing their research skills.
Align rubrics or checklists.	In addition to the research, the rubric also included the group work, presentation, and the cereal-box neatness and creativity. The teacher team decided to instead focus the rubric for this part of the lesson on the research skills, meaning that students could use multiple means of expression to share their research. And, they weren't limited to creating a cereal box.

3. Reflect on how there are scaffolds, tools, or resources for students to select as they work toward that goal. If you recognize that some of the components are not crucial to this part of the lesson, get rid of them or make them one of the flexible options. You may choose to re-craft your goal at this point to really home in on the most important element.
4. Once the goal is clear, you can see how all of the materials, resources, rubrics, and assessments align with the goal.

You may also find it helpful to ask yourselves the following questions once you detangle the goal for a lesson.

- Is the goal clear and understandable to all students? In other words, do they know what they need to know, do, and care about?
- Is the means, or how they need to do the task, embedded in the goal? For example, do students have to write, read, participate by talking aloud, sing, or do pushups? If not, there can be flexibility in how they get there.
- How do your materials, tools, and resources align to and support students to make progress toward that goal?
- How can students make learning choices that help them work toward that goal?

Honor Your Standards

If you use standards in your lessons, this section may be helpful to diving deeper to really break down those standards. If you do not, feel free to move to other sections. Since UDL can align with a standard-based curriculum design, every teaching experience, material, and assessment can be designed to help build and measure student progress toward those standards.

Activity #4: In this activity, educators and administrators will review a set of standards or expectations, identify the exit content and skills learners will need to be successful, and share this information with colleagues or students in a meaningful way to help drive future assessment design. Note that this process aligns with "Backwards Design" (Wiggins & McTighe, 2005). Individually or as a team, take the time and read/review of all your standards. Have a highlighter handy if it's helpful and begin to note all the different knowledge and skills that students have to have to be successful in your lesson.

Scaffolding for Unpacking Standards:

1. Choose a set of standards to analyze. Options: Choose one unit you teach (consider an upcoming unit) and examine those standards. The number of standards will vary based on the subject. If you're looking for a number, try to examine at least five standards, although you may examine many more.

2. Determine your audience. Your audience will impact the format, the level of detail, and the transferability of this project. Options: Your students/ learners, colleagues, your department head, or self.

3. Determine which aspects of the standards require students to "know" and which require learners to "do." Options:

   • Create a table with two or more columns (or use the "Template for Unpacking the Standards Activity" below, or some other model or artistic representation) to differentiate between the knowledge and the skills of the standards.

   • You may choose to add an additional column of prerequisite skills that learners would need before learning the new knowledge outlined in the standard.

   • If the standards are predominantly knowledge standards, note the application of that knowledge (i.e., what are some ways students can apply or practice that knowledge) by creating a list of possible methods, materials, and assessments that students could use whenever working toward knowledge standards. Share your ideas or a sample assignment you are working on with your team.

   • If the standards are predominantly skill-based, consider prerequisite skills to determine what background knowledge is inherent in the skill. Determine different scaffolds or supports that can be available to support your students as they focus on those skills.

Alternative Option to Unpacking the Standards:

One of the principles of proficiency-based learning is that proficiencies include explicit, measurable, transferable learning objectives that empower students. Examine the rubrics already created in your subject areas.

Reflect on the alignment of specific learning objectives to your standards, as described in Table 6.3. Analyze the connection. Do you agree with the interpretation of the standards as they appear in the rubric? Justify your answer. As another option, ask students if they see the connection between the standards and the rubric and then reflect on their answers. If they have suggestions for improvement, do you agree with them? How do these have connection or meaning in their lives?

Table 6.3. Template for Unpacking the Standards Activity

Title or name of the lesson you are reflecting on:			
Audience (who are your learners?):			
Standard(s) addressed in this lesson:	**Is the standard about knowledge (content) or is it skill-based?**	**Pre-requisite content or skills learners will need before learning the standard**	**How do your learning objectives for the given class period or activity align to the standards?**
How do your rubrics and assessments align to your learning objectives?			
How will you gain formative feedback for how students are progressing toward those standards (such as exit tickets or quick check-ins during the class period)?			
How do students see connections between the standards, the objectives, the rubrics, and their lives?			

Transform Tried-and-True Techniques

Once you have thoroughly analyzed your goals, you are ready to begin to transform your tried-and-true techniques. But do not skip out on the goal-setting part; it is essential to UDL implementation and to your Unlearning Cycle.

We have many tried-and-true techniques. Having routines, habits, and tried-and-true techniques are efficient strategies. However, some do not work well. Here, we are going to discuss two of our supposed tried-and-true techniques: differentiated instruction and lesson planning. This section will help clarify how you can unlearn some of the practices associated with each so that you are designing with UDL.

Remember the dinner party analogy? Sometimes when you set a buffet, you may need to guide someone through it, reminding them what they need to eat or encouraging them to try something new. Once the learning buffet is set using UDL, it is easier to differentiate or personalize instruction. Differentiated instruction (DI) responds to different student preferences, readiness, and learning profiles (Tomlinson, 2014). In the buffet analogy, DI helps us create "unique plates" for each student on a given day. UDL recognizes that in a different setting or context, the preferences will change; they are not fixed. The UDL and DI frameworks align; however, the approach is fundamentally different.

Activity #5: Below are two representations that unpack the UDL framework and contrast it to DI. Many educators believe the frameworks are the same, but we hope you see, through one of these representations, how they differ. CAST published an Implementation Brief on the intersections of UDL and DI in 2013. In this brief, the differences are explained as follows:

> DI emphasizes the central role of the teacher to modify content and processes in order to address the needs and learning styles of each student. This responsive learning process can be applied to all activities and assignments and content can be modified so that the materials have relevance and are authentic for each student. There can be flexibility in the assignments and ways students demonstrate what they have learned. DI evaluates a learning style and profile of each student in the construction of activities.
>
> UDL provides an overarching framework for thinking about the design of curricular materials (goals, assessments, materials, methods) for the broadest range of students from the beginning. It is a conceptual shift from thinking about "fixing the student" to "fixing the curriculum." The UDL Guidelines provide suggestions, based on research in the learning sciences,

for how to effectively design curriculum with flexible options that can support a student becoming an "expert learner" (resourceful, strategic, and purposeful) in any context. Options are available for all students as they work to reach the same, high-level goal.

Take a look at Table 6.4 to gain more insight and to develop your own understanding into how DI and UDL are indeed different.

Table 6.4. Differences Between UDL and DI, Adapted From *UDL Now* (Novak, 2016)

Differentiated Instruction	UDL
Reactive	Proactive
Evaluates the student	Evaluates classroom environment and culture.
Adapts script when it's not effective	Intentionally designs options for engagement, representation, and action and expression to reduce those barriers in the scripted lesson.
Retrofits instruction by providing accommodations and modifications	Designs instruction prior to students arrival with embedded goal-driven choices.
Designed for different groups of students based perceived ability or label	Designed for variability, recognizes the context matters for the perceived ability. The "average" learner does not exist.
Plans different learning experiences for students in the margins	Plans for all students in an inclusive environment.
Works around barriers	Reduces barriers
Add your additional ideas here:	Add your additional ideas here:

❋ ❋ ❋

Activity #6: Katie designed a UDL Lesson Review Template (Table 6.5) that helps her reflect on and break some of the old habits of lesson design that were entrenched in practice. UDL lesson plans consider four curriculum components, which make up a complete learning experience: goals, assessments, methods, and materials.

Educators have many options and choices for how to format their lesson design. Below is only one example. Regardless of the format you use, all UDL lesson plans consider proactive design to reduce barriers. In assessments, think about how you are providing formative feedback on a day-to-day basis, but also how you are summatively assessing students as more of a final product or test. Keep the parts that work well; focus on the parts that are barriers for you or your students.

Take time to really analyze a lesson. Remember, you do not need to take this journey alone! You can either work alone or with a small team to build your lesson plan by using the UDL Guidelines to analyze curricular elements.

Table 6.5. UDL Lesson Review Template

	UDL Definition	**Questions for Reflection**
Goals	UDL lessons start with a clear learning goal based on state standards or district proficiencies. Goals include verbs that foster multiple means of action and expression.	• What is the goal of your lesson? • Does it connect explicitly to state standards or district proficiencies? • Does the goal allow for multiple means of engagement, representation, and/or action and expression?
Anticipate variability	Use the UDL Guidelines or jagged learning profiles to anticipate variability you will have in Engagement, Representation, and Action and Expression	• Where do students typically get stuck or frustrated? • Where do you need to reteach?
Methods	There are multiple ways that students can learn content, build background information, and explore the knowledge and skills under study. In UDL students have a choice of which methods they will use.	• Do the flexible methods align with the intended goals? • Do students have a choice about how they will engage with the materials, build knowledge, and access resources?
Materials	Materials are the resources used to present learning content and what the learner uses to demonstrate knowledge.	• Do the flexible materials provided support the intended goal? • Do students have a choice about the materials they will use to learn the material or complete the assessment?

(Continued)

Table 6.5. (*Continued*)

	UDL Definition	Questions for Reflection
Assessments	Assessments gather information about a learner's performance. Often, we think of these as "tests," but they can be any expression of knowledge which allows the educator to determine that the students can meet the goal.	• Do students have a choice about how to express their learning? • Throughout the lesson, is there an opportunity for diagnostic, formative, and summative assessments? • Is the language in the feedback and assessments clear and objective? • Do the assessment criteria align with the intended goal?

Prioritize Engagement

Engagement is critical to learning. Take time to examine the checkpoints under the UDL engagement guidelines to see how you might design options to support student engagement. Really ask yourself why a particular lesson is important, relevant, and meaningful for students to learn. Ask them to make connections and incorporate the ideas they derive from their communities into the lessons.

Activity #7: Visit each other's classrooms and use this UDL Engagement Observation protocol to reflect on how the design supported student engagement.

UDL Engagement Observation Protocol
Pre-questions :

• What is the goal for the lesson or learning experience you are observing?
• What barriers or challenges are anticipated for this lesson? Where have there been barriers to student engagement in this lesson in the past?

You do not need to use all of the UDL Engagement checkpoints in your observation or reflection. Just choose one or two that are most relevant for your focus. In this protocol, be sure to talk to the teacher and students in addition to observing the lesson.

Observation notes or questions:

- How was the goal clarified and made relevant, authentic, or important for students? (7.2 and 8.1)
- How do students have autonomy to make learning choices in the lesson? (7.1)
- What are some of the threats or distractions in a lesson? What options to reduce such threats or distractions in the environment are there for all students to use? (7.3)
- How are there various resources available for students to choose in order to work toward the goal? (8.2)
- In what ways are there options for collaboration? How is community fostered in the design of the lesson or in the classroom routines? (8.3)
- How is feedback given—Teacher to student, student to student, or student to self? How does it focus on the process of learning? Is it frequent and formative feedback? (8.4)
- In what ways are high expectations communicated for all students in the process of learning? (9.1)
- What options are there for students to use if they feel challenged or frustrated in a lesson? (9.2)
- In what ways are students encouraged to reflect on their own learning process and choices in the lesson? (9.3)

Go for Expert Learning

Regardless of the age of your students, every one of them can become an expert learner. UDL provides the framework to build toward expert learning. You may need to start with access, as students must be able to perceive, recruit interest, and physically act to initiate learning. Ultimately however, we want them to be able to self-regulate, develop strong levels of comprehension, and be able to set their own learning goals and self-monitor their progress. Within our individual disciplines expert learning looks different. Whether a kindergartener making observations and formulating a hypothesis or a professional scientist, we can start to take those core disciplinary skills, habits, and practices (many of which are addressed in standards) and build them explicitly into our lessons.

❋ ❋ ❋

Activity #8: UDL Expert Learner Reflection. Use Table 6.6 based on CAST's definition of expert learners, to reflect on your discipline or on the content area in terms of expert learning. Not all expert learning elements need to be present at all times, but approach the learning as being about building and growing toward that.

You can also reflect on how you are progressing as an expert learner with your UDL understanding or other professional learning pursuit. Another option is to

Table 6.6. Looking for Expert Learning

Identify the Discipline, Domain, Subject Area, or Skill You Are Focusing on, such as Writing, Mathematics, Cooking, Running, Music, and so forth. Choose 1-2 Checkpoints to Focus on at a Time.
UDL Engagement Principle: Expert Learners Who Are Purposeful and Motivated How do students: • make choices that align with the goals and learning needs? • engage in authentic, relevant problems or issues in the discipline? • recognize what elements are distracting for their work and take steps to minimize them? • know when and how to collaborate? • utilize relevant resources for meeting the demands of the task? • understand what to do to help them persist through challenges? • receive and incorporate feedback on their progress? • self-reflect on their progress and make adjustments as needed? • focus on challenging problems and believe they can achieve their goals?
UDL Representation Principle: Expert Learners Who Are Resourceful and Knowledgeable How do students: • know how to gain access to the pertinent content and information? • recognize when they are lacking background and can figure out how to gain it? • learn and incorporate relevant language and symbols of the domain? • organize relevant background in ways that deepen transfer of understanding to new contexts? • use their background to gain additional background understanding?

UDL Action and Expression Principle: Expert Learners Who Are Strategic, Goal-Directed

How do students:

- choose methods that best enable them to demonstrate or show their questions or understanding?
- know when they need to use additional tools or technologies to develop their skills?
- express and communicate their learning to others?
- know their strengths and weaknesses and how to find resources to build on their weaknesses?
- understand how to monitor their progress and redirect as needed as they evaluate their progress toward reaching the end goal?
- demonstrate best practices within the field (such as writing, researching, and painting)?

access Appendix C for the UDL Progression Rubric (Novak & Rodriguez, 2018) to view the lifetime journey toward ensuring that all students—and educators—are progressing toward expert learning.

Activity #9: In this reflection, use table 6.7 where you can focus on how the design of the environment helps students build autonomy so they feel comfortable taking risks and ownership of their learning. Notice how this UDL focus is on the design, which includes the goals, assessments, materials, methods, and physical environments. There are also components that the teacher and students contribute, but this activity focuses on the design of the environment.

Table 6.7.

Autonomy Reflection Sheet. Ask Yourself:
• How does the flexibility of the design of my lesson support learners to feel safe enough to take risks inherent in choice?
• How does the design support learners in feeling a positive connection to the class?
• How does the design help learners get to know each other?
• How are students valued for their individual strengths?
• How does the design help learners work with each other?
• How does the design offer opportunities for learners to choose, do, and review?
• How does the design offer flexible time options for learning?

Make It Yours

At this point, we have shared strategies to take action within each of the stages of the Unlearning Cycle. Here are our recommendations for attaining deeper understanding about UDL and UDL implementation:

- Don't try to do it alone. Set up team collaboration and regular times to meet and discuss UDL goals and barriers, variability, and context. Share your work and strategies with other educators. Visit each other's classrooms. Brainstorm around the design of the different lessons you are creating during a department or PLC meeting. Use models such as instructional rounds, where a team visits many different classrooms with a common focus on comparing and discussing teaching and learning (Marzano, 2011).
- Start small. Perhaps you make just one change in the environment or focus on goals. Realize that, even as we try this new approach to teaching and learning, we will still fall back on old patterns and habits. For instance, we will still catch ourselves lecturing to everyone with no alternative to the verbal content. We will still ask all our students to write an essay, even though the goal is understanding the content.
- Take the time to disentangle your goals so that you really know what you are focusing on at the various points of a lesson or unit. This is one of the most important steps for lesson design.
- Keep referencing the UDL Guidelines. They will seem overwhelming at first, but they are the road map to deep understanding of learning, variability, and barriers.

Over time, a subtle transformation can begin to take place in your classrooms and schools. You will see a shift to more goal-directed, intentional planning and communication in service of engaged and expert learning—for all students.

In Conclusion: Diffusion of Innovation

Remember the story from our introduction? One hundred sailors go out to sea. Fifty die of scurvy, and it takes the British Navy two hundred years to endorse the idea of giving their sailors daily doses of three teaspoons of lemon juice. Reflect on some of the data from your school. Whom is school not working for?

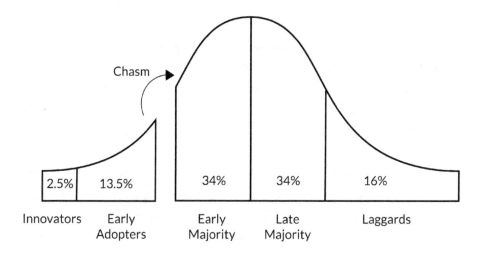

Chasm

| 2.5% | 13.5% | 34% | 34% | 16% |

Innovators | Early Adopters | Early Majority | Late Majority | Laggards

We don't have two hundred years to meet the needs of all our students. We need to do it now. If you care about education, you're likely obsessed with why some innovations are able to beat this time line, to bring about change rapidly, whereas most others are forever relegated to oblivion. The figure above depicts the adopter categories in the Diffusion of Innovation model. You will note the large gap between early adopters and the early majority. This gap, referred to as "the chasm," is where most ideas go to die.

Malcolm Gladwell, the best-selling author of *The Tipping Point* and other books, explains that the chasm is the tipping point for innovation. He points to the Law of the Few (Gladwell, 2000) to explain why this chasm between the introduction and the adoption of an innovation exists. The Law of the Few explains why the success of an innovation is dependent on the types of people who are its innovators and early adopters. In UDL, we aren't past the tipping point, so it is critical that we, as educators and passionate practitioners, find people who possess the gifts that the Law of the Few have. We need to transform our teams now, or we will have to wait another two hundred years. Captain Lancaster made a mistake. He didn't have the right people. We can't make that same mistake. What the Captain did have, however, was lemon juice—and we have UDL. If we want to overcome the existent barriers and ensure that all students have opportunities to build engagement and become expert learners regardless of variability, we have to become one of the few. Every one of us.

It's tempting to think we have come far from the days when students were seated by IQ, but the truth is that we haven't. In many classrooms, we still seat our students according to label, and this affects the quality of education they receive. We still believe that ability grouping is "tried-and-true" despite evidence to the contrary. Students still know who the "top" group is and when they get moved "down." They may perceive from a very early age what their ability is/is not, so we have to design better.

Our students don't need labels to get what they deserve. Instead, they should be able to self-advocate, have their voices heard, and make things as challenging as they need to be, and teachers must collaborate and become facilitators of that work. So many people ask, is UDL good for talented students? Is it good for special-education students? Let us be clear. UDL is the best practice and can meet the needs of all students when we have high expectations for their achievement. In order to achieve this, we have to have higher expectations for ourselves and believe that we can meet the needs of all kids when they're together.

For Us, It's Personal

For us, Universal Design for Learning has become personal. As educators, we believe in the potential power of every child and challenge ourselves to find things about them that we love, often in face of the accusation, "Well, you like everyone." Clearly, we were meant to be in education.

Katie is the proud mother of four amazing children. She has three sons and an amazing, firecracker daughter named Aylin. Aylin is a whirlwind of charisma, impulsivity, hilarity, anger, and compassion. At the age of six, that sweet girl was diagnosed with combined-type ADHD and anxiety, but that was no surprise. From the time she was eighteen months old, Katie knew she would have to adapt and be a much different parent than she would be for the boys.

"UDL helped me and my husband to build a home and a family where Aylin can thrive. Although she can be combative, obstinate, and angry, when she is empowered to be self-directed and channel that grit, she is unstoppable. In our house, ADHD is her superpower. But what about school?

"At her school, a district staffed with my colleagues embraces UDL. Aylin has opportunities throughout her school day for physical action, to make her own choices, to collaborate with her peers, and to customize her own journey. But UDL isn't just about Aylin.

"Her twin brother, Brecan, is in the same class. Brec would be successful in any classroom. He is the poster child for the 'mythical average learner' who can be compliant and respectful despite the circumstances. He will do anything you ask, even if he is bored out of his mind and his eyes glazed over like a donut. Luckily, Brecan enjoys every minute at school. If you ask him what is his favorite class he will tell you it's WIN block, which is the 'What I Need' block for students to self-assess their progress, determine their goals for improvement, and engage in the skills and strategies that are most meaningful to them with the teachers facilitation and support.

"Aylin's best friend's name is James. James loves to run and is a champion at tag. His favorite food, which he discovered recently, are lemon-filled Oreos. Aylin and James love art, playing Legos, and running in incessant circles outside. James has fragile X syndrome. The National Fragile X Foundation defines fragile X syndrome as 'a genetic condition that causes intellectual disability, behavioral and learning challenges and various physical characteristics.' I want to be the first to say that these children are so much more than their disabilities. If these kids don't have the opportunity to experience success like Brecan, who arrives at school ready to learn, our schools and systems are not effective.

Even though these three children, Aylin, Brecan, and James, and their twenty classmates, are wildly different from one another, they can all be successful because of UDL.

"As a teacher and a mom, I refuse to believe in a world where our children cannot be educated together," says Katie. "For me, it is become a personal fight. As I said, UDL has gotten personal."

If it is so clear from both a social-justice perspective and an educator's heart that all students deserve the opportunity to learn with and from one another in rigorous environments that allow them to personalize their journey, why is it taking so long for UDL to take off? Why are so many kids like Aylin and James completely separated from their peers, in classrooms without subject-matter experts and, more importantly, their peers?

This is a question that keeps us up at night. If you're reading this, we imagine it keeps you up too. As we travel around the world, we partake in too many conversations with administrators and teachers who tell us that children are still segregated and separate because they "can't" access a classroom with their peers. We need to change the narrative. The truth is that we can't provide an education that meets the needs of all students, and that is a travesty.

We could list a thousand reasons why students struggle in inclusive classrooms, including academic deficits, social-emotional dysregulation, and behavioral challenges. We could also provide you with reasons why people think that some students are better off when they are separated into gifted programs. We can continue to use reasons that are categorized into variables that relate to the kids, their families, or our system. Or we can make a change and have higher expectations for all kids. The evidence of UDL is indisputable and yet often ignored. But why?

In this book, we have proposed several reasons why it is hard to change. Cognitive load can lead us to fall back on simpler, routine decisions—our "tried-and-true" that we have always done and that help us in our days consumed by balancing teaching responsibilities, administrative duties, daily communications, meetings, grading, and preparation for the next day.

Gladwell's work (2000) suggests another reason why UDL may not always catch on. Every innovation needs three key individuals to close the gap: a *salesperson*, a *maven*, and a *connector*. Think about your own UDL journey. You will probably realize that there are three people who inspired you and brought you into this movement for good.

The Salesperson, the Maven, and the Connector

A salesman must have all the charm and skills to convince people to do anything. If you think about your school or your organization, there are always one or two people that have the ability to get people on board or to step out of their comfort zones to try something new. Ironically, the same salesmen can also convince people not to try new things, and so salespeople are important to have in your corner. If you know you possess this ability to inspire people to try new things, use it. And know that a true salesman will always try to close the sale.

Katie's husband, Lon, has an MBA and is a very successful salesman. He is optimistic, motivated, and inspiring. Katie says, "He once told me that a good day is when he talks to hundred people and only ninety-nine hang up or yell at him. It's a good day because there are only ninety-nine more people to win over, instead of a hundred." In sales, you have to keep trying because you believe in your product. To win over one's clients, the goal is to get to know them individually and continue to reach out to them over and over again until one gets results.

If you're a salesperson by nature, ask yourself: Are you trying hard enough to scale Universal Design for Learning? If you're frustrated with trying to sell UDL and you're not getting results, it's because you haven't won your clients over, *yet*. In sales, you need charm, persistence, and self-direction—a little of UDL itself.

In our presentations around the globe, we hear the same objections all the time: "My colleagues just won't do this"; "There's already an initiative overload. I can't introduce one more thing"; "We don't have time or money, or kids can't just do this." Listen, salespeople: you can make excuses, or you can make a difference. Salespeople have to make a difference. If every salesperson in UDL converts a single believer, we will begin to build a bridge to cross the chasm.

If Captain Lancaster had had a salesperson on his side, he would have been selling lemon juice like hotcakes, but alas, our friend Lancaster wasn't a salesperson. He also wasn't a maven.

Salespeople can't do it alone. Mavens are information seekers and spreaders; they are our book readers, our researchers, and our thinkers. Mavens diffuse an innovation through their vast knowledge of the subject matter. Colleagues consider them experts because they are well read, well researched, and well respected for that knowledge.

We think of David Rose, one of the founders of CAST, as the ultimate maven. CAST was founded by a team of four brilliant educators and innovators—and all of them played essential roles in developing an organization that would go on to change the world for all learners. But when people think of UDL, they usually think first of David Rose, because he was obsessed with spreading the UDL message far and wide so everyone had access to it. He wrote papers and books, lectured at conferences, and for decades was the face of CAST as the chief education officer and co-executive director. He also rarely took individual credit for anything. He always focused on the collaboration and the importance of the ideas, not the person who developed them.

If you are a maven, people look up to you because of your knowledge, and so it is your duty to learn as much as you can about UDL to spread that knowledge to others. Read every peer-reviewed article that is published, stay current on Twitter and by reading the blogs of UDL experts. Keep up-to-date on CAST's website and follow its social media. The more you know, the more you can impart, and because people look up to you for your ideas, you have a very important role.

On social media today, we call these mavens *influencers*. An influencer has an established credibility in a specific area and can persuade others because of this expertise. Clearly Captain Lancaster didn't have much clout in the British Navy yards, because if he had, his little lemon juice experiment would have taken off faster.

Last, a team that is meant to cross the bridge together will have a connector. A connector knows everyone. It is the connector's mission to get to know people and connect them to others. While Allison finds that CAST to be a network hub of UDL and as the site that innovates and iterates the content around the UDL Guidelines and where international leaders convene to discuss and research UDL, it is actually the students who are our connectors. Regardless of the site, anywhere in the world, educators connect us to the individual students who inspire us to change. The more we keep our students in mind, the more connected we will be to our work, and the more inspired we will be to connect with others.

We are selling UDL because these days there is an act of civil war against our children who are most at risk of failing. We cannot allow educators and systems to decide that our students are not capable and then prevent them from accessing the very experiences that will allow them change the trajectory of their lives. We have not crossed the chasm, but we will. The tipping point is in our reach if we all commit to becoming "the few."

It is time to focus on our design, starting with our learning goals. It is not that students "these days" do not have attention or are not engaged. It is our design that must inspire attention and interest. Flipping the conversation to how all students can succeed beyond our expectations through our design is empowering.

The stories that inspire us are the ones we hear from educators across the country. It's often a story that has a similar structure: "Let me tell you about this student . . . the one I did not think could/would do this . . . and all I did was change this one part of the lesson . . . and *that* student achieved beyond my expectations . . . and now this student is so different in my class."

We also become inspired when we recall some of the founding stories from CAST. For example, one of our favorites is the story of Matthew, a boy who had locked-in syndrome and could not communicate or physically move most of his body. His mind, however, was incredibly strong. CAST developed a switch tool that reduced the physical communication barrier, and he was able to participate academically in school with his peers. We are confident that in every learning experience there is a "switch" of some kind for each and every student that we can include by design. Finding these strategies and different pathways is the most fun to discover, but we can only discover it through a rich process of unlearning.

So, please, embrace the Unlearning Cycle in your own practice and inspire others to do the same. Hold true to your core beliefs that all students are capable of learning. If we didn't all believe this, we wouldn't have become teachers. All our students have amazing potential to be engaged, expert learners, and only through unlearning what we know and trading up for new models of thinking, teaching, and learning can we give all students the education they deserve. They will surpass our expectations every time.

Reflect:

- Who has been your salesperson, maven, or connector? Which will you strive to be as you share your UDL journey with others?
- Record at least two actions you will take as a result of this book. Design a plan for yourself: what you will do, whom you will work with, and what you will see as change. Diagram it, add images to it, come up with a mascot or theme song that will encourage you to go onward!

UDL Lemon Herb Cocktail

in honor of Captain James Lancaster

The Herb

Muddle 4 large basil leaves in the bottom of your glass.
Don't like basil? Try mint, cilantro, or a sprig of rosemary.
Leaving out the herb is also ok!

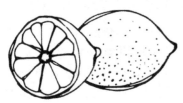

The Fruit

Add 2 tsp. fresh-squeezed lemon juice into the glass.
Lemons make you pucker? Try 1/4 cup freshly squeezed
watermelon juice, or 1/4 cup cucumber juice.

The Base

Pour 1 cup of plain seltzer in your glass with ice.
Want to kick it up a notch? Mix 6 oz. seltzer with 2 oz. vodka or
gin. Can't do bubbles? Still water works too!

The Sweetener

Mix in 1/4 tsp. rose water and 2 Tbsp. simple syrup.
Rose water taste like soap to you? Leave it out or substitute a
dash of your favorite bitters. If using vodka or gin in your base,
try using 1 oz. Elderflower Liqueur instead of simple syrup.

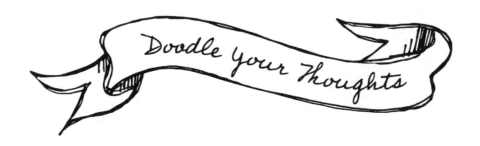

References

Al-Fadhli, H., & Singh, M. (2006). Teachers' expectancy and efficacy as correlates of school achievement in Delta Mississippi. *Journal of Personnel Evaluation Education, 19,* 51–67.

Anderson, M. (2016). *Learning to choose, choosing to learn: The key to student motivation and achievement.* Alexandria, VA: ASCD.

Cooper, H., Robinson, J. C., & Patall, E. A. (2006). Does homework improve academic achievement? A synthesis of research, 1987–2003. *Review of Educational Research, 76*(1), 1–62.

Dale, A., & Hagren, E. (2017). Annenberg Foundation videos. Retrieved from https://www.learner.org/courses/neuroscience/common_includes/si_flowplayer.html?pid=2377

Duhigg, C. (2012). *The power of habit: Why we do what we do in life and business* (Vol. 34, 10th ed.). New York, NY: Random House.

Gladwell, M. (2000). *The tipping point: How little things can make a big difference.* Boston, MA: Little, Brown.

Grotzer, T. (2012). *Learning causality in a complex world: Understandings of consequence.* New York, NY: R&L Education.

Hattie, J. (2009). *Visible learning: A synthesis of over 800 meta-analyses relating to achievement.* New York, NY: Routledge.

Longfield, J. (2009). Discrepant teaching events: Using an inquiry stance to address students' misconceptions. *International Journal of Teaching and Learning in Higher Education, 21*(2), 266–271. Retrieved from https://www.isetl.org/ijtlhe/pdf/IJTLHE732.pdf

Maltese, A., Tai, R., & Fan, X. (2012). When is homework worth the time? Evaluating the association between homework and achievement in high school science and math. *High School Journal, 96*(1), 52–72.

Marzano, R. J. (2011). The art and science of teaching: Making the most of instructional rounds. *Educational Leadership, 68*(5), 80–82. Retrieved from http://www.ascd.org/publications educational-leadership/feb11/vol68/num05/Making-the-Most-of-Instructional-Rounds.aspx

Merton, R. (1948). The self-fulfilling prophecy. *Antioch Review, 8,* 193–210.

Meyer, A., Rose, D. H., & Gordon, D. (2014). *Universal design for learning: Theory & practice.* Wakefield, MA: CAST.

Novak, K. (2016). *UDL Now: A teacher's guide to applying UDL in today's classrooms.* Wakefield, MA: CAST.

Novak, K., & Rodriguez, K. (2018). *UDL progression rubric.* Wakefield, MA: CAST. Retrieved from http://castpublishing.org/wp-content/uploads/2018/02/UDL _Progression_Rubric_FINAL_Web_REV1.pdf

Posner, G. J., Strike, K. A., Hewson, P. W., & Gertzog, W. A. (1982). Accommodation of a scientific conception: Toward a theory of conceptual change. *Science Education, 66*(2), 211–227.

Rogers, E. M. (1962). *Diffusion of innovations.* New York, NY: Free Press of Glencoe.

Rose, T. (2016). *The end of average.* New York, NY: HarperCollins.

Rosenthal, R., & Jacobson, L. (1968). *Pygmalion in the classroom: Teacher expectation and pupils' intellectual development.* New York, NY: Holt, Rinehart & Winston.

Tannahill, R. (1989). *Food in history.* New York, NY: Crown.

Tomlinson, C. A. (2014). *The differentiated classroom: Responding to the needs of all learners.* Alexandria, VA: ASCD.

Wiggins, G. P., & McTighe, J. (2005). *Understanding by design.* Alexandria, VA: ASCD.

Willingham, D. (2018). How many people believe learning styles theories are right? [blog post]. Retrieved from http://www.danielwillingham.com/daniel -willingham-science-and-education-blog/how-many-people-believe-learning -styles-theories-are-right-and-why

Yazzie-Mintz, E. (2010). *Charting the path from engagement to achievement: A report on the 2009 High School Survey of Student Engagement.* Bloomington, IN: Center for Evaluation and Education Policy.

Appendix A
Books and Articles to Learn More About UDL

Note that this book is not an introduction to UDL. We recommend these books to build an overview of UDL:

- *UDL Now! A Teacher's Guide to Applying Universal Design for Learning in Today's Classrooms* by Katie Novak (2016, Wakefield, MA: CAST).
- *Design and Deliver: Planning and Teaching Using Universal Design for Learning* by Loui Lord Nelson (2013, Baltimore, MD: Paul Brookes).
- *Your UDL Lesson Planner: The Step-By-Step Guide for Teaching All Learners* by Patti Ralabate (2016, Baltimore, MD: Paul Brookes).
- *Dive into UDL: Immersive Practices to Design for Expert Learning* by Kendra Grant and Luis Perez (2018, Washington, DC: ISTE).
- *Universal Design for Learning: Theory and Practice* by Anne Meyer, David H. Rose, and David Gordon (2014, Wakefield, MA: CAST).

This book is not about UDL implementation, for that we recommend:

- *Universally Designed Leadership: Applying UDL to Systems and Schools* by Katie Novak and Kristan Rodriguez (2016, Wakefield, MA: CAST).
- *UDL: Moving from Exploration to Integration*, edited by Elizabeth Berquist (2017, Wakefield, MA: CAST).

Also look for many new titles being added every year by CAST Publishing. Visit www.castpublishing.org to learn more.

Appendix B
UDL Guidelines

The Universal Design for Learning Guidelines

CAST | Until learning has no limits

Provide multiple means of **Engagement**	Provide multiple means of **Representation**	Provide multiple means of **Action & Expression**
Affective Networks — The "WHY" of Learning	Recognition Networks — The "WHAT" of Learning	Strategic Networks — The "HOW" of Learning

Access

Provide options for **Recruiting Interest**
- Optimize individual choice and autonomy
- Optimize relevance, value, and authenticity
- Minimize threats and distractions

Provide options for **Perception**
- Offer ways of customizing the display of information
- Offer alternatives for auditory information
- Offer alternatives for visual information

Provide options for **Physical Action**
- Vary the methods for response and navigation
- Optimize access to tools and assistive technologies

Build

Provide options for **Sustaining Effort & Persistence**
- Heighten salience of goals and objectives
- Vary demands and resources to optimize challenge
- Foster collaboration and community
- Increase mastery-oriented feedback

Provide options for **Language & Symbols**
- Clarify vocabulary and symbols
- Clarify syntax and structure
- Support decoding of text, mathematical notation, and symbols
- Promote understanding across languages
- Illustrate through multiple media

Provide options for **Expression & Communication**
- Use multiple media for communication
- Use multiple tools for construction and composition
- Build fluencies with graduated levels of support for practice and performance

Internalize

Provide options for **Self Regulation**
- Promote expectations and beliefs that optimize motivation
- Facilitate personal coping skills and strategies
- Develop self-assessment and reflection

Provide options for **Comprehension**
- Activate or supply background knowledge
- Highlight patterns, critical features, big ideas, and relationships
- Guide information processing and visualization
- Maximize transfer and generalization

Provide options for **Executive Functions**
- Guide appropriate goal-setting
- Support planning and strategy development
- Facilitate managing information and resources
- Enhance capacity for monitoring progress

Goal

Expert learners who are...

Purposeful & Motivated	Resourceful & Knowledgeable	Strategic & Goal-Directed

udlguidelines.cast.org | © CAST, Inc. 2018 | Suggested Citation: CAST (2018). Universal design for learning guidelines version 2.2 [graphic organizer]. Wakefield, MA: Author.

Appendix C
UDL Progression Rubric

Based on the CAST UDL Guidelines (2018)

UDL Progression Rubric
Katie Novak & Kristan Rodriguez

Provide multiple means of Engagement

		Emerging	Proficient	Progressing Toward Expert Practice
Provide options for recruiting interest (7)	Optimize individual choice and autonomy (7.1)	Offer choices in what students learn (e.g., "choose a country to study" rather than "study France"), how students learn (e.g., use books, videos, and/or teacher instruction to build understanding), and how they express what they know (e.g., "you can create poster or write paragraph").	Encourage students to choose from multiple options to determine what they learn (guided by standards), how they learn, and how they express what they know. Encourage students to suggest additional options if they can still meet the standard.	Empower students to make choices or suggest alternatives for what they will learn, how they will learn, and how they will express what they know in authentic ways. Free them to self-monitor and reflect on their choices with teacher facilitation and feedback but not explicit direction.
	Optimize relevance, value, and authenticity (7.2)	Offer options that highlight what your learners deem relevant, valuable, and meaningful. For example, you may conduct a student survey and then make instructional decisions based on areas of interest.	Encourage students to share what is relevant, valuable and authentic to them and encourage them to suggest teaching and assessment options that would allow them to meet a defined standard, tying in their interests, culture, and personal strengths. This may be done in a weekly exit ticket, or class discussion, for example.	Empower students to make connections between the content, their own interests, and then push them to link their understanding to authentic real-world scenarios and authentic assessments so they can design their own learning experiences with coaching from the teacher. For example, instead of assigning a lab or giving students the choice of two labs, empower them to design their own lab based on the standard and their scientific interests.
	Minimize threats and distractions (7.3)	Offer options that reduce threats and negative distractions for everyone to create a safe space in which learning can occur. For example, have choices for seating, collaborative work, and clear PBIS expectations.	Collaborate with students to define classroom norms and PBIS expectations and encourage students to help to design the classroom so there are multiple options for seating, collaboration, etc.	Empower students to self-advocate and collaborate to identify threats and distractions and then create creative solutions that will allow them to excel. Student voice drives the environment.

CAST | Until learning has no limits

Engagement

		Emerging	Proficient	Progressing Toward Expert Practice
Provide options for sustaining effort and persistence (8)	Heighten salience of goals and objectives (8.1)	Build in "reminders" of both goals and their value. For example, write standards on the board and/or at the top of assessments and projects.	Encourage students to collaboratively discuss goals in light of students' own passions and interests and to choose from various options to reach the goals.	When given the learning standard, have students create personal goals for how they will learn the content, express the content, and challenge themselves throughout the process.
	Vary demands and resources to optimize challenge (8.2)	Provide options for students to learn content with clear degrees of difficulty. For example, "Explore one of the following resources to learn about the Civil War..." and there may be a rigorous primary source document and a video.	Provide multiple options for students to learn content with clear degrees of difficulty which will require them to reflect on the standard and their own strategy for learning. For example, "Choose two of the following six resources to learn about the Civil War..." and there may be rigorous primary source documents, summary documents, videos, and/ or a podcasts from a professor.	Empower students to select their own content and/or own assessments, based on standards, and encourage them to collaborate to add to the multiple options offered to challenge themselves and identify appropriate resources that connect to their interests and passions.
	Foster collaboration and community (8.3)	Provide opportunities for students to learn how to work effectively with others. For example, create cooperative learning groups with clear goals, roles, and responsibilities.	Develop a classroom that values collaborative groupwork. Students construct their own groups and create their own group norms, responsibilities, etc. and students often seek out and work with diverse partners.	Create a classroom culture where students work together to define goals, create strategies, provide feedback to each other and push each other with mastery-oriented feedback while building integrative thinking.
	Increase mastery-oriented feedback (8.4)	Provide feedback that guides learners toward mastery rather than a fixed notion of performance or compliance. For example, provide feedback that encourages the use of specific supports and strategies in the face of challenge.	In addition to providing emerging feedback, empower students to provide mastery-oriented feedback to each other to support specific improvement and increased effort and persistence.	Implement proficient practice and also empower students to use mastery-oriented feedback independently to self-reflect, self-direct, and pursue personal growth in areas of challenge.

CAST | **Until learning has no limits**

Engagement

		Emerging	Proficient	Progressing Toward Expert Practice
Provide options for self-regulation (9)	Promote expectations and beliefs that optimize motivation (9.1)	Teach students about the power of perseverance and use language and feedback that will allow all students to see themselves as capable learners.	Foster conversations with students to develop relationships and make authentic connections and use their personal passions and interests to help inspire them and push them toward success.	Create a classroom culture where students are empowered and able to support their own self-talk and support one another's positive attitudes toward learning.
	Facilitate personal coping skills and strategies (9.2)	Offer reminders, models, and tools, to assist learners in managing and directing their emotional responses. For example, use stories or simulations to demonstrate coping skills. Offer options for stress release such as alternate seating, fidget tools, mindfulness breaks, etc.	Empower students to deal with difficult challenges by allowing them to choose from multiple strategies to regulate their learning (e.g., a relaxation corner, put on headphones, take a walk).	Encourage students to self-reflect, accurately interpret their feelings, and use appropriate coping strategies and skills to foster learning for themselves and their classmates.
	Develop self-assessment and reflection (9.3)	Provide students with tools so they are reflecting on their learning through rubrics, self-assessment, etc.	Offer multiple models and scaffolds of different self-assessment techniques so students can identify and choose ones that are optimal. For example, these might include ways to collect, measure, and display data from their own behavior and academic performance for the purpose of monitoring growth.	Create a culture where students consistently reflect on the learning process and assessments so they become self-directed learners who grow over time.

CAST | **Until learning has no limits**

Representation

	Emerging	Proficient	Progressing Toward Expert Practice
Provide options for perception (1)			
Offer ways of customizing the display of information (1.1)	Create resources and materials that address variability and meet the needs of more students (e.g., large size print, additional white space, visuals).	Create resources and materials that students can access electronically. Allow students to use their devices to interact with textual, visual and audio information so they can personalize, take notes, increase/decrease size/volume, etc.	Empower students to choose resources and materials that best meet their needs (e.g., watch a video OR explore a handout) so they can personalize their learning themselves without explicit direction from a teacher.
Offer alternatives for auditory information (1.2)	Provide an embedded option for any information presented aurally. For example, use closed-captions when playing a video.	Provide multiple options for students to choose alternatives to learn content so they don't have to rely on auditory information (e.g., closed captions for video or the choice of reading a text).	Empower students to select auditory alternatives as well as provide them with a framework to locate additional, reputable resources to build their understanding (e.g., resources on how to determine if a website or author is credible).
Offer alternatives for visual information (1.3)	Provide an embedded option for students so they don't have to rely on visual information. For example, reading aloud to the class while they read along.	Provide multiple options for students to choose alternatives to learn content so they don't have to rely on visual information (e.g., listen to audiobook instead of reading or choose to work with teacher for short presentation).	Empower students to select alternatives to visual information as well as provide them with a framework to locate additional, reputable resources to build their understanding (e.g., resources on how to determine if a website or author is credible).

CAST | Until learning has no limits™

Representation

Provide multiple means of **Representation**

		Emerging	Proficient	Progressing Toward Expert Practice
Provide options for language, mathematical expressions, and symbols (2)	Clarify vocabulary and symbols (2.1)	Translate idioms, archaic expressions, culturally exclusive phrases, and slang. For example, explicitly teach vocabulary to students using definitions, visuals, explanations, and examples.	In addition to emerging practice, provide students with explicit instruction in context clues so they can independently learn words unfamiliar to them.	Empower students to use available resources to work collaboratively to determine authentic ways to use relevant vocabulary.
	Clarify syntax and structure (2.2)	Clarify unfamiliar syntax (in language or in math formulas) or underlying structure (in diagrams, graphs, illustrations, extended expositions or narratives). For example, highlight the transition words in an essay.	Provide students with resources that will allow they themselves to clarify syntax and structure (such as dictionaries, math reference sheets, thesaurus, etc.)	Empower students to preview material under study, highlight areas in need of clarification, and choose appropriate resources to build knowledge and understanding.
	Support decoding of text, mathematical notation, and symbols (2.3)	Provide direct instruction, prompts, and scaffolded materials for students who struggle to comprehend information. Or provide alternatives, such as visuals, to support this understanding.	Provide strategies and materials (e.g., math reference sheets, context clue strategies, and so forth) that lower barriers to understand and help students figure out notations, symbols, or problems.	Empower students to independently utilize learned strategies to decode text, mathematical notation, and symbols.
	Promote understanding across languages (2.4)	Provide alternative presentations of material, especially for key information or vocabulary. For example, make key information in the dominant language (e.g., English) also available in the first languages of learners with limited-English proficiency. Also, use images AND words, show opposites, etc.	Provide students with access to tools such as apps, websites, and dictionaries to translate material under study and to collaboratively build understanding.	Empower students to independently utilize options to translate material under study, collaborate to build understanding using tools, apps, etc.
	Illustrate through multiple media (2.5)	Present key concepts in one form of symbolic representation (e.g., an expository text or a math equation) with an alternative form (e.g., an illustration, diagram, video, etc.)	Present students with multiple options and symbolic representations to make meaning and allow them to choose options to build comprehension.	Empower students to choose effective resources from multiple options with multiple representations so not all students are required to learn from the same resources.

CAST | **Until learning has no limits**

Representation

		Emerging	Proficient	Progressing Toward Expert Practice
Provide options for comprehension (3)	Activate or supply background knowledge (3.1)	Provide all students with background information on content using direct instruction with options for visuals, audio, etc.	Provide students with options that supply or activate relevant prior knowledge, or link to the prerequisite information elsewhere. For example, use advanced organizers (e.g., KWL methods, concept maps) and then encourage students to select resources that will allow them to build appropriate background knowledge.	Empower students to determine gaps in their own background knowledge and then select appropriate resources to build that knowledge in order to achieve the goals of a lesson. For example, begin with a diagnostic assessment and ask students to reflect and create a strategy for filling in gaps in learning.
	Highlight patterns, critical features, big ideas, and relationships (3.2)	Provide explicit cues or prompts to help students recognize the most important features in information. For example, teach students to use outlines, graphic organizers, highlighters, etc.	Provide students with options and multiple strategies to support recognition of the most important features in information. For example, allow them to use outlines, graphic organizer, highlighter, word cloud apps, and other organizing tools.	Empower students to self-reflect to determine the most effective strategies for highlighting critical information and independently select the strategies that allow them to support recognition of patterns, critical features, big ideas, and relationships.
	Guide information processing, visualization, and manipulation (3.3)	Provide all students with materials, strategies, and tools to support processing and visualization. Tools include manipulatives (i.e, counting cubes), glossaries, graphic organizers, and more.	Provide students with options of multiple materials, strategies, and tools to use to support processing and visualization, such as the option to make visual notes, use technology to locate images, and/or select and use manipulatives, etc.	Empower students to self-reflect and independently choose the most appropriate materials, strategies, and tools to guide information processing, visualization, and manipulation, searching for additional tools and strategies, if necessary.
	Maximize transfer and generalization (3.4)	Model explicit strategies students can use to transfer the information they have to other content areas and situations. For example, show how the knowledge could be used in another class or be used to make comparisons across content in the class (such as text to text comparisons).	Provide options for meaningful transfer, such as interdisciplinary projects, where students can make authentic connections and apply knowledge in meaningful ways in other content areas and in authentic situations.	Encourage students to apply knowledge and skills learned in class to enhance their understanding of content, design of their own authentic projects, and express their knowledge and understanding in authentic, real-world scenarios.

UDL Progression Rubric | Page 6
Novak & Rodriguez | ©2018

CAST | Until learning has no limits™

Action & Expression

		Emerging	Proficient	Progressing Toward Expert Practice
Provide options for physical action (4)	Vary the methods for response and navigation (4.1)	Provide more than one option for the methods used for response and navigation within the same assignment. For example, some students may use IPads while others write by hand.	Provide multiple options for the methods used for response and navigation within the same assignment. For example, some students may use IPads, different writing utensils, keyboards, voice recognition software, etc.	Empower students to use their own devices to respond to and interact with materials for all assignments (e.g., options to use headphones, keyboards, manipulatives, joysticks, etc.).
	Optimize access to tools and assistive technologies (4.2)	Allow some students to use assistive technologies for navigation, interaction, and composition if required by an IEP or 504.	Provide multiple options for all students to use assistive technology like IPads, voice recognition, and 1:1 devices regardless of variability.	Empower students to assess the need for and choose technologies that work for them to provide additional, personalized options to express their knowledge and skills.
Provide options for expression and communication (5)	Use multiple media for communication (5.1)	Provide more than one way to answer on assessments so students can express their understanding without barriers. Taking a traditional test may be one option, but so, too, could be an oral presentation or writing an essay.	Provide students with multiple options to express their understanding—and let them suggest some ways of being assessed, so they understand that showing what they know is the point rather than how well they perform on a particular kind of test. Students may choose to express their understanding in text, audio, video, multimedia, live presentations, and many other ways.	Let students reflect on a standard or a set of competency or proficiency-based rubrics, and then independently create authentic and innovative products that allow them to demonstrate their mastery of the standard.
	Use multiple tools for construction and composition (5.2)	Provide the choice of more than one tool or strategy to help students express their knowledge. For example, allow students to compose a response using traditional pen and paper or allow them to create a multimedia presentation on their device.	Provide multiple tools and strategies to help students express their knowledge. For example, allow students to compose a response using traditional written methods, blogging software, or multimedia tools such as ThingLink or Emaze.	When provided with a task, or when independently creating an authentic product, students are empowered to self-reflect and select tools and materials that will support their learning and challenge them to strive for rigorous options to express knowledge and skills in accessible, engaging ways using, and then building upon, the tools they were exposed to in class.
	Build fluencies with graduated levels of support for practice and performance (5.3)	Implement a scaffolding model from teacher-directed to collaborative groups to independent work, slowly releasing responsibility to students. For example, in collaborative work, assign team members specific tasks and monitor their progress before moving to independent work or move from teacher-directed instruction to Socratic seminars.	Provide options for support and scaffolding throughout the learning process and encourage students to choose resources that allow them to build their own knowledge while working in collaborative groups and working independently. In collaborative groups, for example, encourage students to self-select roles; in class discussions, have students collaborate to design the rules and structures.	Empower students to create challenges that let them productively struggle to reach rigorous goals and use supports as tools to help them to make improvements rather than making things "easier." Encourage students to provide feedback and drive teacher instruction; encourage them to define roles and expectations for group work that include routine monitoring and reflection.

CAST | Until learning has no limits

Action & Expression

		Emerging	Proficient	Progressing Toward Expert Practice
Provide options for executive functions (6)	Guide appropriate goal-setting (6.1)	Provide clear goals to students so it's clear what they must do to meet or exceed expectations. For example, post standards on the board and on assignments, and articulate those standards and goals throughout the lesson.	Create conditions for learners to develop goal-setting skills. For example, provide students with standards on the board and on assignments, but also provide models or examples of the process and product of goal setting so all students can develop personalized goals while working toward standards.	Encourage students to create personalized learning plans that include goals that align as well as action plans and strategies that optimize personal strengths while addressing individualized areas of challenge.
	Support planning and strategy development (6.2)	Facilitate the process of strategic planning. For example, provide all students with checklists for tasks, due dates, and planning templates to keep students organized.	Facilitate the process of strategic planning. For example, provide students not only with organizational tools but with scaffolds they need to create personalized strategies to meet their goals.	Empower students to self-reflect, self-assess, and create personalized action plans to achieve their identified goals. For example, encourage students to reflect on how much time and resources they need to perform selected tasks and then encourage them to make personal due dates and task lists to reach their goals.
	Facilitate managing information and resources (6.3)	Provide scaffolds and supports to act as organizational aids for students. For example, provide all students with templates for note-taking.	Provide exposure to multiple scaffolds, supports, and resources that act as organization aids, such as a variety of graphic organizers or different strategies for note-taking.	Empower students to self-reflect, self-assess, and independently choose the most appropriate supports and resources that will allow them to organize information and resources so they can achieve their identified goal(s).
	Enhance capacity for monitoring progress (6.4)	Provide formative feedback tools to students so they can monitor their own progress. For example, provide students with assessment checklists, scoring rubrics, and multiple examples of annotated student work/performance examples.	Provide multiple opportunities for students to receive feedback from the teacher, peers, and themselves using a variety of tools such as assessment checklists, scoring rubrics, and exemplars.	Empower students to use multiple resources, including teachers and peers, to consistently reflect on their performance, collect feedback, and revise their work to promote and highlight growth.

UDL Progression Rubric | Page 8
Novak & Rodriguez | ©2018

CAST | **Until learning has no limits**

Acknowledgments

From Allison

For me, inspiration for this book began in graduate school when my professor, Tina Grotzer, challenged me to think more deeply about learning, unlearning, and conceptual change—and about why change can be so hard, even when we know better. In my current work with teachers and administrators, I observed this firsthand: we know that school does not work for so many students; however, change in teaching and school practices is hard. In my observations and work at CAST, and in collaboration with amazing colleagues such as Rachel Currie-Rubin, Niel Albero, Jayne Bishoff, and more, I began to deepen my thinking about conceptual change, teacher practice, and Universal Design for Learning. Tina, Rachel, Niel, and Jayne, thank you for planting the seeds for this book.

It was at a UDL conference that I heard Katie Novak present about the Three Teaspoons of Lemon Juice, and we immediately began to brainstorm about how to pull the theories together. Bryan Dean, thank you for helping us frame the thinking—you are one of the most compassionate advocates for students I know. Katie, thank you for this collaboration. Every time we talk or text, I am inspired by your depth of knowledge. Your energy and passion for the work inspires so many. I am honored to be one of them. A high-heeled "cheers" to many more years of collaboration.

David Gordon, thank you for your partnership in this journey—not only for publishing this work, but also for supporting my writing early in my career at CAST. You have done so much to promote many voices from the UDL field to ensure learning has no limits. Billie Fitzpatrick, your insights and advice deepened my learning and writing. Thank you.

To the many leaders from the emerging UDL field, thank you for continuing a movement initiated and inspired by David Rose, Anne Meyer, Grace Meo, Skip Stahl, and others who seek to reduce unnecessary barriers to learning. We owe it to future generations to keep working to transform our education system and curricula to be designed equitably and in service of challenging, meaningful, and expert learning for every individual.

To my family, thank you for being there through busy schedules, new routines and transitions, and moments of celebration. Whether we are on top of a mountain, enjoying dessert, or just watching a sunset, you are my roots. Griffin and Ella, you each inspire me each day to keep learning and unlearning so I will grow as an individual and as your mumma/madre. I love you.

From Katie

This book is Lucky #7 and I am so lucky to have written it with Allison Posey. The UDL community has welcomed me from the beginning and I am so grateful to get to work with amazing, beautiful people like Allison. AP—you are a mentor, a friend, and an amazing collaborator and hopefully, there is more writing in our future.

To Bryan Dean, thanks for inspiring this book and being a part of our journey. You were instrumental in getting us started and you continually up our "coolness" factor. Without you, we couldn't get away with calling ourselves "dope." We are both rooting for you to be the next on the CAST publication list as the world needs a UDL/Hype Cycle mash-up.

To David Gordon and Billie Fitzpatrick—for being the best darn editors on the planet. I am so grateful that you respect me enough to say things like, "This is a great book . . . starting with Chapter 4. You don't need anything before that." Having critical friends who are wordsmiths and muses is such a blessing.

There are so many people in my UDL family that push my thinking and help me better myself every day. Some of the many who have inspired me and pushed me this year are Sean Bracken, Mirko Chardin, George Couros, Joni Degner, Tesha Fritzgerald, Luis Perez, Kristan Rodriguez, Zach Smith, and Mike Woodlock. I am not sure what I would do without you all.

To L-Train, aka, Laura Chesson, Big Boss: Thank you for dealing with all of my quirks, crazy ideas, and squirrel-like attention span. I love working with and for you and especially appreciate all of your colorful analogies!

Always, so much love and appreciation to the peeps who make my world go round: Lon, Torin, Aylin, Brec, and Boden. Lon, being your wife is the most magnificent adventure. There isn't a thing I would change. I still think that Match.com should hire us for their commercials—clearly everyone would be talking about how I'm the funny one. Kiddos, if you weren't mine, I would wish that you were. I love you best.

About the Authors

Allison Posey

Allison Posey, MEd, is a curriculum and design specialist at CAST, the education nonprofit that developed the Universal Design for Learning framework, and the author of *Engage the Brain: How to Design for Learning that Taps into the Power of Emotion* (ASCD, 2018).

At CAST, Allison participates in the development of content and materials that support learning opportunities for all individuals through UDL implementation. She leads national and international professional learning programs that strive to integrate current understandings from brain science into instructional practices. She also hosts a free webinar series for educators with the goal of sharing best practices around equity and inclusion.

Prior to coming to CAST, Allison was a life science teacher in high school and community college settings, teaching courses such as genetics, anatomy, physiology, biology, neuroscience, and psychology. She received a degree in Mind, Brain, and Education from Harvard Graduate School of Education where she also worked as a teaching fellow for courses such as Educational Neuroscience and Framing Scientific Research for Public Understanding. She holds a Certificate in Fine Arts from the Maryland Institute of Art.

Katie Novak

Katie Novak, EdD, is an internationally renowned education consultant as well as a practicing leader in education as an assistant superintendent of schools in Massachusetts. With seventeen years of experience in teaching and administration and an earned doctorate in curriculum and teaching from Boston University, Katie designs and presents workshops both nationally and internationally focusing on implementation of Universal Design for Learning (UDL) and universally designed leadership.

Dr. Novak is the author of the best-sellers *UDL Now! A Teacher's Guide to Applying Universal Design for Learning in Today's Classrooms* (CAST, 2016) and *Innovate Inside the Box: Empowering Learners Through UDL and the Innovator's Mindset* (with George Couros, Impress, 2019), and five other books, including this one. Novak's work has been highlighted in many publications including *Language, NAESP Principal, ADDitude, Commonwealth, Principal Leadership, District Administrator, ASCD Education Update*, and *School Administrator*, and the Huffington Post.

Novak's work in UDL has impacted educators worldwide as her contributions and collaborations have built upon the foundation for an educational framework that is critical for student success.

Index

Page numbers followed by *f* and *t* indicate figures and tables respectively.

T

U

V